Sacramental Streams

Sacramental Streams

*Lutheran Baptismal Theology
from the Old Testament into the New*

RICHARD DAVENPORT

Foreword by Kent Burreson

RESOURCE *Publications* · Eugene, Oregon

SACRAMENTAL STREAMS
Lutheran Baptismal Theology from the Old Testament into the New

Copyright © 2025 Richard Davenport. All rights reserved. Except for brief quotations in critical publications or reviews, no part of this book may be reproduced in any manner without prior written permission from the publisher. Write: Permissions, Wipf and Stock Publishers, 199 W. 8th Ave., Suite 3, Eugene, OR 97401.

Resource Publications
An Imprint of Wipf and Stock Publishers
199 W. 8th Ave., Suite 3
Eugene, OR 97401

www.wipfandstock.com

PAPERBACK ISBN: 979-8-3852-3534-6
HARDCOVER ISBN: 979-8-3852-3535-3
EBOOK ISBN: 979-8-3852-3536-0

01/09/25

Scripture quotations are from the ESV® Bible (The Holy Bible, English Standard Version®), © 2001 by Crossway, a publishing ministry of Good News Publishers. Used by permission. All rights reserved. The ESV text may not be quoted in any publication made available to the public by a Creative Commons license. The ESV may not be translated in whole or in part into any other language.

Quotations from *For the Life of the World: Sacraments and Orthodoxy* are copyright © 1973 by St. Vladimir's Seminary Press. Used by permission.

Quotations from *Of Water and the Spirit: A Liturgical Study of Baptism* are copyright © 1974 by St. Vladmir's Seminary Press. Used by permission.

Quotations from *Our Father* are copyright © 2002 by St. Vladimir's Seminary Press. Used by permission.

Quotations from *Liturgy and Life: Lectures and Essays on Christian Development Through Liturgical Experience* are copyright © 2006 by the Orthodox Church in America. Used by permission.

Quotations from *The Book of Concord: The Confessions of the Evangelical Lutheran Church* are copyright © 2000 Fortress. Used by permission.

Quotations from *Luther's Works Volumes 31–54* copyright © 1999 by Fortress. Used by permission.

Quotations from *Luther Works Volumes 1–30, 69* © 1958–2009 Concordia Publishing House. Used with permission. All rights reserved. cph.org.

The Bible and the Liturgy by Jean Daniélou © 1956 by the University of Notre Dame. Reprinted by permission of Notre Dame Press.

This book is dedicated to my son, Paul,
who I had the special privilege of baptizing into God's family.

Contents

Foreword by Kent Burreson		ix
Abbreviations		xiii
Introduction		xv
1	Baptism: The Sacrament of Grace	1
2	Baptism: The Sacrament of Creation	8
3	Baptism: The Sacrament of Vocation	18
4	Baptism: The Sacrament of Eternity	38
5	Baptism: The Sacrament of Holiness	48
6	Baptism: The Sacrament of Passage	61
7	Baptism: The Sacrament of Re-Creation	71
8	Baptism: The Sacrament of the Spirit	78
9	Baptism: The Sacrament of Discipleship	87
10	Baptism: The Sacrament of Worship Restored	94
11	The Worship Service—Where Disciples are Trained	118
Conclusion		122
Bibliography		125

Foreword

As a child I grew up in a family house that sat on a ridge above a wooded area. Through the middle of those green-in-summer and white-in-winter woods flowed a docile stream. We, the children in my neighborhood, loved to walk, pick rocks, and splash in that stream in the heady days of summer, when life seemed to stretch out as an endless canvas before us. In that stream we found refreshment for our spirits and a source of joy for our hearts. *Sacramental Streams: Lutheran Baptismal Theology from the Old Testament into the New* by Richard Davenport provides just such a stream for the reader to splash and play in, the stream of their baptism into Christ.

But that belies the problem. To splash and play in a stream, you need some knowledge of why and how to do so. But people don't know the rationale or the means for exploring the baptismal stream. As Davenport indicates, "many Christians can no longer explain the significance of Baptism beyond the most basic assertion that it provides the forgiveness of sins." Yet, that significance, or signification, is the very water in which the Christian fish needs to swim. Without it they can't fully appreciate their baptism and or know how to live a baptismal life as "one redeemed by Christ the crucified." In his monumentally important book *The Bible and the Liturgy*, the French liturgical scholar Jean Daniélou identified the same problem back in 1951:

> Theology defines the sacraments as "efficacious signs,"—this being the sense of the scholastic saying *(significando causant)*. But, as things are today, our modern textbooks insist almost exclusively on the first term of this definition. We study the efficacious causality of the sacraments, but we pay very little attention to their nature as *signs*. It is, therefore, to this aspect of the sacraments in particular that the chapters of this book will be devoted. We shall study the significance of the sacramental rites, and, more generally, that of Christian worship. But the purpose of this study is not

> simply to satisfy our curiosity. This question of the sacraments as signs is of fundamental importance for pastoral liturgy. Because they are not understood, the rites of the sacraments often seem to the faithful to be artificial and sometimes even shocking. It is only by discovering their meaning that the value of these rites will once more be appreciated.[1]

Clearly little has changed regarding awareness of sacramental signification among the baptized people of God. In the lineage of Daniélou's work, *Sacramental Streams* seeks to soak the people of God in the meaning and significance of their baptismal waters.

So how does the book achieve this? Two words summarize the method: *biblical typology*. *Sacramental Streams* is a work that explores biblical typology in the baptismal liturgy. Daniélou compellingly describes biblical typology:

> That the realities of the Old Testament are figures of those of the New is one of the principles of biblical theology. This science of the similitudes between the two Testaments is called *typology*. And here we would do well to remind ourselves of its foundation, for this is to be found in the Old Testament itself. . . . The New Testament, therefore, did not invent typology, but simply showed that it was fulfilled in the person of Jesus of Nazareth. With Jesus, in fact, these events of the end, of the fullness of time, are now accomplished. He is the New Adam with whom the time of the Paradise of the future has begun. In Him is already realized that destruction of the sinful world of which the Flood was the figure. In Him is accomplished the true Exodus which delivers the people of God from the tyranny of the demon. . . .. The eschatological typology of the Old Testament is accomplished not only in the person of Christ, but also in the Church. Besides Christological typology therefore, there exists a sacramental typology, and we find it in the New Testament.[2]

Understanding baptismal significance means immersing oneself in the place of that biblical and sacramental typology. *Sacramental Streams* explores those Old Testament, New Testament, and ritual types from the baptismal and Sunday eucharistic liturgies, soaking God's children in the baptismal waters of Jesus.

---

1. Daniélou, *The Bible and the Liturgy*, 3.
2. Daniélou, *The Bible and the Liturgy*, 4–5.

Foreword

Therein lies the treasure of this book: conforming the reader to Christ. *Sacramental Streams* aims to do so through such primary biblical typology and imagery: creation and the flood; vocations of prophet, priest, and king; anointing and holiness; circumcision and baptism as the eighth day of new creation; Passover and the passage to the greater day of the Eschaton; re-creation; and new birth in the Spirit. Through this typological exploration the reader becomes aware of how they have entered a new way of life, the first fruits of a new creation. As Daniélou says, even into the Kingdom of God:

> The sacraments were thought of as the essential events of Christian existence, and of existence itself, as being the prolongation of the great works of God in the Old Testament and the New. In them was inaugurated a new creation which introduced the Christian even now into the Kingdom of God.[3]

Sacramental streams that inaugurate one into the Kingdom.

Davenport unfolds these types and images through the language of two essential theologians in the West and the East: Martin Luther and Alexander Schmemann. While written from a Lutheran perspective, this work in sacramental imagination draws upon the tradition of the church catholic. Luther's intent is always to make faith live in the saving promises of God in Christ Jesus. Schmemann's intent is to make us more like Christ in our daily being, lived out of the sacraments themselves. Here is a whole new world to explore. As Schmemann says in his study of baptism, *Of Water and the Spirit*:

> And the source, always living and life-giving, is precisely *Baptism*—Baptism not as one isolated "means of grace" among many, . . . but Baptism as that essential act by which the Church always reveals and communicates her own faith, her "experience" of man and the world, of creation, fall and redemption, of Christ and the Holy Spirit, of the new life of the new creation, as indeed the source of the whole life of the Church and of the Christian life of each one of us.[4]

A fundamental way of knowing the shape of Christian life is by exploring that experience, that sacramental experience. And the baptismal experience is a rich one. A rich experience to which *Sacramental Streams* opens the door. As Davenport concludes:

---

3. Daniélou, *The Bible and the Liturgy*, 17.
4. Schmemann, *Of Water and the Spirit*, 151–52.

Foreword

The wealth of biblical imagery and meaning behind Baptism gives the church an endless fountain with which to confront sin and offer God's gracious restoration. The forgiveness given in Baptism does so much more than we might first expect. It is an endless, ever-present gift from God that strikes us differently every time we contemplate its richness. With the wealth of baptismal grace to meditate on, we will never cease to find God's consolation and wisdom wherever we find ourselves in life.

May *Sacramental Streams* lead you, O reader, into the riches of such lifelong meditation on the baptismal flood.

Kent Burreson
Concordia Seminary, St. Louis, Missouri

Abbreviations

AC   Augsburg Confession

Ap   Apology of the Augsburg Confession

FC   Formula of Concord

LC   Large Catechism of Martin Luther

NT   New Testament

OT   Old Testament

SA   Smalcald Articles

SC   Small Catechism of Martin Luther

SD   Solid Declaration of the Formula of Concord

Introduction

DISCUSSIONS ABOUT BAPTISM—ITS MEANING and purpose—go back to the very earliest days of the church. Paul mentions it in many places throughout his epistles. Peter references it as well. Jesus Himself has a detailed conversation about it with His disciples before He ascends into heaven, leaving thoughts of Baptism with them.

It is safe to say Baptism has been a part of the church from its very infancy. The early fathers explained at length their interpretation of the spiritual and symbolic activity that takes place within the baptismal rite. Theologians such as Augustine, Tertullian, and others wrote extensively about Baptism, making allegorical and typological connections to varying degrees. Martin Luther spent a great deal of time debating the purpose and application of the sacraments with the other reformers of his day.

After the Reformation, when society moved into the era of modernism, much of the understanding of Christian laity, and even clergy, was pared back to bare essentials. In the many centuries since the days of the early fathers, a great deal of the ritual activity that used to be woven into the baptismal rite is no longer understood and much has become lost. Many Christians can no longer explain the significance of Baptism beyond the most basic assertion that it provides the forgiveness of sins.

There is no one factor at fault for this loss. The Eastern Church has become mired in the ritual activity of Baptism, such that some of the fundamentals have been lost or obscured. The Western Church, for those denominations that retain any sacramental awareness of Baptism, the fundamentals may be there, but they are left without any application to ongoing Christian life and faith.

In order to bring back a more complete understanding of Baptism I will draw on the thoughts of both the East and the West. Alexander Schmemann and Martin Luther are two important representatives of East and

Introduction

West, respectively, and both wrote extensively on the work and purpose of the sacraments and their connection to Christian life. Their comments will show that nothing in this book is truly new. What this book presents is a collection of theological insights that have been around since the early days of the church. While they may have been forgotten or fragmented, they are a part of our rich sacramental tradition as well.

For most Lutherans, the sacramental theology of Martin Luther will already be well known. Even a cursory read through his Small Catechism shows how important he understands the sacraments to be. The work of Schmemann will probably be unfamiliar to many in the Lutheran church. The Eastern Orthodox church simply is not one we find ourselves in conversation with as readily as other Christian traditions. Thus, their theological perspective tends to be less well known. Though much of what Schmemann says here sounds very compatible with Lutheran theology, the broader view of his work shows that he never strays out of Eastern Orthodoxy.

He, like the Eastern Orthodox church as a whole, does not operate with the Lutheran concept of Law and Gospel as his primary theological framework. Instead, he thinks in terms of *theosis*, being made more like Christ. He utilizes the Eastern Orthodox understanding of the sacraments to drive his understanding of their work and purpose. In his mind, the primary purpose of the sacraments is to make us more like Christ. Thus, rites such as ordination and marriage function as sacraments since they conform us to Christ's image in different ways.

While our definition of sacrament is different and is rightly focused on the promise of God's grace, Schmemann's view of the sacraments as conforming us to Christ has much to offer, not so much from a justification standpoint but from a sanctification standpoint. Schmemann has a great deal to say about the continuing work of God through the sacraments in the life of God's church and thus, when seen from a Lutheran perspective, is a valuable voice in any discussion of the purpose and work of the sacraments. These two, together with occasional comments from other worthy theologians, will help us truly grasp the impact this wondrous mystery has in the life of the church.

1

Baptism: The Sacrament of Grace

BEFORE WE CAN DELVE into what Baptism does, we must first establish what Baptism is. As I said in the introduction, the church's understanding of Baptism has become both more simplistic and more convoluted. Though our theology has not officially changed, our practice and application have suffered. In the first place, general understanding of Baptism has receded, so that now the discussions about Baptism throughout much of Lutheranism begin and end with what we are told about it in Luther's Small Catechism.

In his Small Catechism, Luther focuses his attention on the grace offered through Baptism and its power to justify the sinner. He wants there to be no doubt that this is the primary work of Baptism. Baptism truly is a "means of grace." It is one of the vehicles God uses to convey His grace and forgiveness to His people. He makes a promise to each and every person who is baptized and He stakes His name and reputation on the promise made there. Every baptized Christian is claimed as His own through adoption into His family, grafted into a place we previously had no right to be associated with.

At the same time, Baptism also has a special relationship to God's Word. The Lutheran reformers define the term "sacrament" in Ap XIII:

> If we define the sacraments as rites, which have the command of God and to which the promise of grace has been added, it is easy to determine what the sacraments are, properly speaking. For humanly instituted rites are not sacraments, properly speaking, because human beings do not have the authority to promise grace. Therefore signs instituted without the command of God are not

sure signs of grace, even though they perhaps serve to teach or admonish the common folk. Therefore, the sacraments are actually baptism, the Lord's Supper, and absolution (the sacrament of repentance).[1]

The assumption is that Baptism is necessary because it is a guarantee that faith is created as the Holy Spirit enters into the life of the one being baptized. While Baptism is often linked to salvation language throughout the New Testament, that does not make salvation language synonymous with faith. The themes associated with Baptism tend to be distinct from the themes that relate specifically to faith. While Peter does say Baptism saves, we must be careful not to conflate this with the creation of faith.

Like Baptism, faith is also an unmerited gift. God offers it to us and we either receive it willingly or we cast aside that gift and all of the benefits that go with it. The New Testament does not change how faith is created; it merely brings the object of that faith into focus. In the Old Testament, a believer trusted in the promise of the coming Savior; now, we trust in the Savior who has already come. In either case, it is that Word of promise relating God's grace given through the death and resurrection of Christ that the Spirit is active through that Word. As Paul says in Romans: "if you confess with your mouth that Jesus is Lord and believe in your heart that God raised Him from the dead, you will be saved" (Rom. 10:9). He also says, "no one can say 'Jesus is Lord' except in the Holy Spirit" (1 Cor. 12:3). The Holy Spirit is always active wherever the Word is proclaimed and is active in bringing faith to those who hear it.

Luther also rejects the idea that faith is necessarily created in Baptism. Rather, he argues Baptism and faith are separate events and that faith may not be there at all when one is baptized. A small piece of his argument against rebaptizing states this:

> Now [Jesus] commands that all the world shall receive it. On the strength of that command (since none is excluded) we confidently and freely baptize everyone, excluding no one except those who oppose it and refuse to receive this covenant. If we follow his command and baptize everyone, we leave it to him to be concerned about the faith of those baptized. We have done our best when we have preached and baptized.[2]

---

1. Kolb et al., *The Book of Concord*, 219.
2. Luther, *Luther's Works, Vol. 40*, 258.

Baptism: The Sacrament of Grace

Faith must be there to receive what is given in Baptism, but Baptism is intended to build on faith. Baptism is not primarily directed at creating faith. Luther further comments on this in LC IV:

> We bring the child in the conviction and hope that it believes, and we pray that God may grant it faith [Luke 17:2; Ephesians 2:8]. But we do not baptize it for that reason, but solely because of God's command. Why? Because we know that God does not lie [Titus 1:2]. I and my neighbor and, in short, all people, may err and deceive, but God's Word cannot err.[3]

We baptize based on the command of Christ. Any other gifts God may choose to bestow are left to Him. We are also careful to affirm that faith can certainly be created here. God's Word is active within Baptism. Without the Word, there is no sacrament. God claims His child and adds His name to each person who receives His gifts in Baptism.

That said, God's Word is encountered in many places. Wherever God's Word is preached and proclaimed, His promises are offered. These promises are offered to all who hear, whether young or old. The most basic element of faith is the trust we have in the promises God makes. In Romans 10, Paul tells us, "So faith comes from hearing, and hearing through the word of Christ" (v. 17). The statement is simple and straightforward. God makes His promise to each of us, whether directly through His proclaimed Word or through the sacraments. That promise calls on the hearer to trust Him.

The rationalist argument that infants and others who are unable to fully comprehend God's Word are unable to come to faith through it is simply not expressed in Scripture. In places such as Luke 10:21, Jesus remarks on how God has revealed Himself to little children instead of the wise and understanding. The Psalmist also says, "Upon you I have leaned from before my birth; you are he who took me from my mother's womb" (Ps. 71:6). He expresses faith and trust in God at a point where no higher order understanding would be possible. This lack of understanding has no effect on even an unborn child's ability to trust in God.

That leads to the question as to what role greater understanding plays in relation to faith. In this case, learning and growth in understanding are part of living a life in faith. That growth in understanding forms the sanctification side of faith. As we will see later, it follows Christ's command to make disciples, for teaching is a necessary part of the life of discipleship.

---

3. Kolb et al., *The Book of Concord*, 464.

Thus Baptism, by virtue of being a singular event in the life of the Christian, becomes an undeniable point of assurance. Prior to Baptism, one might be given to wonder whether all sins were truly forgiven or whether one was truly righteous in the eyes of God. At the font, God pours a lifetime of grace into a single moment. There is nothing more to doubt. God promises that the one who enters the water is forgiven and made righteous. Whatever came before the water is washed away and the promise made in Baptism continues to stand from that point on. Whenever someone is tempted to doubt God's grace, he need only look back at that point at the font and know with certainty that he has received it. Now, as the Christian confesses his sins and looks for absolution, that confession is shaped by what Baptism has given him. Baptism shows him what he should be doing and what his life should look like. His contrition then contains the desire to return to the vocations given him in the sacrament and the grace to carry out the responsibilities necessitated by those vocations.

With an understanding of what Baptism is, we can now turn our attention to what Baptism is doing. To see what makes Baptism unique and special, we must compare it with other places where God offers His grace and forgiveness. For most of us Christians, including Lutherans, Baptism is not something we know much about. That is not to say we do not know anything about it at all, but it is not a topic we spend much time thinking about in any great depth. Lutherans are typically taught a summary of what the Bible says about Baptism, as well as what Luther says about in the Small Catechism, but rarely does the preaching or theological discussion of Baptism go much beyond that. That means much of what the Bible says to explain the fuller purpose of Baptism goes unexplored.

In order to see what makes Baptism unique, we must contrast it with other ways in which God is granting His grace. Typically, the most common place we receive God's grace is through absolution. In most Lutheran churches, Confession and Absolution are a part of every Divine Service. The rite of Confession and Absolution typically occurs shortly after the service begins. The congregation confesses before God that they are sinners and are unable to earn their own salvation. The pastor, as representative of Christ, announces Christ's own words of forgiveness. You are truly and completely forgiven, and your sins are wiped away. What is more, in Matthew 18, Jesus makes clear God's forgiveness is there as often as you need it. Even before the service is over, you could confess further sins to God in your heart and know they are forgiven. If that is the case, then you may wonder why you need the forgiveness and grace that God bestows in Baptism since you are already forgiven in the worship service. You are forgiven anytime you ask God for mercy and grace. He promises to give it to you. So why do you really need Baptism?

Absolution is the free and full forgiveness of all sins. Christ forgives all sins and died for all sins. No sin is so great or so heinous that He will not forgive it. In his explanation of confession in his Small Catechism, Martin Luther asks:

> "*What is Confession?*"
>
> Answer: Confession consists of two parts. One is that we confess our sins. The other is that we receive the absolution, that is, forgiveness, from the confessor as from God himself and by no means doubt but firmly believe that our sins are thereby forgiven before God in heaven.[4]

Forgiveness is already there in Confession and Absolution. That may seem to leave Baptism in an odd spot. The idea that Baptism might give *more* forgiveness does not really fit. Either I am forgiven by Absolution or I am not, and if I am not, the Absolution does not really save me from anything. It means I still have sin in there somewhere and eternal condemnation is still coming for me.

The Eastern Orthodox Church sees chrismation, anointing with holy oil, as a sacrament, but one which is intrinsically tied to Baptism and often done within the same rite. In that regard, Schmemann highlights part of the problem we face with Baptism:

> We know already that these definitions [of the sacraments] were rooted in a particular understanding of *grace* and of *means of grace*; hence the "definition" of Chrismation as the sacrament which bestows on the newly baptized the gifts (Χαρίσματα) of the Holy Spirit, i.e. grace, necessary for his Christian life—a definition given in virtually all theological manuals, Eastern as well as Western. But the real question, the one that the Orthodox theologians while fighting on two fronts—the Roman and the Protestant—did not raise, is whether this very definition is a sufficient or even an adequate one. For as it stands, it clearly makes the Western "dilemma" unavoidable. Indeed, either the grace received in Baptism makes any new gift of grace superfluous (the Protestant solution), or the grace bestowed in the second sacrament is an entirely

---

4. Kolb et al., *The Book of Concord*, 360. Italics in original.

"different" grace and its bestowing, in virtue of this difference, not only can but even must be "disconnected" from Baptism (the Catholic solution).[5]

The Orthodox theological framework is a bit different from what those of us in the West typically operate with. His assessment of Protestant theology is also rather broad-brush, since there is substantial variation among Protestant denominations. Nevertheless, his point is still worthy of consideration. Protestant sacramental theology might substitute Holy Communion for chrismation in Schmemann's statement, in that its grace is either superfluous and adds nothing to what Baptism or Absolution do or it is completely disconnected from them. The same can be said then of Baptism and the usefulness of the forgiveness it claims to give.

We know God offers His forgiveness freely and His word of absolution does exactly what it says. So, we cannot very well say that forgiveness is ineffective. Those who confess their sins receive His forgiveness. There is no reason to doubt His promise of forgiveness. However, if that is the case, what does that mean for Baptism? The God who declares, "For I will forgive their iniquity, and I will remember their sin no more" (Jer. 31:34), cannot then require something further to forgive those same sins without invalidating that free forgiveness.

Since Baptism and Absolution are offering the same grace, we might be led to think that there truly is no difference between them. However, as we will explore, there are a great many themes woven throughout the Old and New Testaments that connect specifically to Baptism. Peter, for instance, tells us that Baptism corresponds to the Flood:

> For Christ also suffered once for sins, the righteous for the unrighteous, that he might bring us to God, being put to death in the flesh but made alive in the spirit, in which he went and proclaimed to the spirits in prison, because they formerly did not obey, when God's patience waited in the days of Noah, while the ark was being prepared, in which a few, that is, eight persons, were brought safely through water. Baptism, which corresponds to this, now saves you, not as a removal of dirt from the body but as an appeal to God for a good conscience, through the resurrection of Jesus Christ... (1 Peter 3:18–21)

Peter states plainly that the Flood is telling us about Baptism. The Flood might tell us a great many things about God's general plan of salvation, but

---

5. Schmemann, *Of Water and the Spirit*, 77. Italics in original.

it also describes something specific about Baptism. That means, while Baptism may not differ from Absolution or even Communion in its role as a means of God's grace and a method God uses to justify the unrighteous sinner, it still has a unique place in the life of God's people. Each of the themes we will discuss has something to say, not just about how God's forgiveness and grace are given in Baptism, but about Baptism's role in sanctification, the ongoing work of Baptism in the life of the individual Christian and the Church as a whole.

It is with this in mind that we examine the different stories and themes that are essential to understanding Baptism. To that end, we shall dig through many of the pieces scattered throughout Scripture to see if we can build a fuller picture of what Baptism is meant to be and, in doing so, come to a deeper awareness of what it is meant to do in the life of the church. An examination of Baptism and its themes will show that the grace found in Baptism is neither superfluous nor disconnected from absolution. The ongoing work Baptism accomplishes in us beautifully complements absolution, making both important in their own ways and ensuring neither can be a complete substitute for the other. Without a thorough understanding of Baptism, the church runs the risk of eliminating Baptism's very purpose and stunting the growth of God's people.

2

Baptism: The Sacrament of Creation

THE FLOOD IN GENESIS sets the tone for later events and is probably the most profound event in the Old Testament relating to Baptism. God pronounces the entire world guilty of unbelief, with the exception of Noah and his family. God directs Noah to build an ark and promises that the people and animals in the ark will survive the destruction of all other terrestrial life on the planet. Obviously, there is a lot of water involved. That alone should make us at least consider the possibility that Baptism figures in here.

God saving His people through water seems like an easy connection to make regarding Baptism. Luther references the Flood in his baptismal prayer, typically called his Flood Prayer: "Almighty, eternal God, who according to your strict judgment condemned the unbelieving world through the flood and according to your great mercy preserved believing Noah and the seven members of his family . . ."[1] God promises salvation through water. Noah and his family believe and are saved. The relationship seems pretty clear, and it is already a potent analogy for what happens in Baptism.

Sadly, even Lutherans, who pride themselves on their use of the sacraments, rarely dig further into the story than that. We hear Peter's brief statement and nod sagely: "when God's patience waited in the days of Noah, while the ark was being prepared, in which a few, that is, eight persons, were brought safely through water. Baptism, which corresponds to this, now saves you, not as a removal of dirt from the body but as an appeal to God for a good conscience" (1 Pet. 3:20–21). While it is true God is saving

---

1. Kolb et al., *The Book of Concord*, 373.

His people through water, there is so much more going here. There is so much more God has to teach us about Baptism in these few chapters in Genesis.

To better understand the importance of the Flood, we first need to understand its context. Genesis 6 tells us:

> The Lord saw that the wickedness of man was great in the earth, and that every intention of the thoughts of his heart was only evil continually. And the Lord regretted that He had made man on the earth, and it grieved Him to His heart. So the Lord said, "I will blot out man whom I have created from the face of the land, man and animals and creeping things and birds of the heavens, for I am sorry that I have made them." (vv. 5–7)

Already in six chapters we go from a world God looks at and calls "very good" (Gen. 1:31) to a world so full of evil the only option is to wipe out everything but Noah, his family, and a few animals, and start over again.

The world that God called "very good" also started with water. Genesis 1:2 informs us the earth begins as a formless ball of water, pure and undisturbed. As the Master Artisan, God takes this featureless substance and begins crafting it into what He wants it to be. He calls light into being to illuminate His workspace. He begins dividing it out, creating land, then plants, and so forth. Finally, on the sixth day, He forms the crown of His creation out of the earth and places Adam and Eve in a pure and perfect paradise.

At some point after that, Adam and Eve reject God's command and the invisible corruption of sin spreads throughout the entire world, subjecting everything to death. Time passes and we arrive at Noah, with the corruption of sin now pervading everything to such an extent that only Noah and his family are considered righteous. God is grieved at the state of His creation and declares His just judgment against it. Noah builds the ark and he, his family, and the animals climb in. Then the waters pour down from above and rise up from beneath.

The extent and the manner by which God blots out all life on the planet is important. Each day of creation is undone in the Flood. The world becomes all but peaceful as the terrible storm is unleashed across the whole face of the earth. People and animals sink beneath the waves. Dry land disappears, taking with it all of the plants. The waters that had been separated to make the waters above and the waters below on day two of creation merge together once more. The heavenly bodies and even light itself are all but blotted out in the forty-day deluge. Noah and his family are sitting on the boat as they watch creation rewinding over the course of the storm, until finally the storm passes. There on the ark looking out as the storm had finally ceased, one would see nothing but a formless ball of water, pure and undisturbed.

To say then that the Flood teaches us about Baptism becomes a much bigger affair than a simple declaration that God saves us through water. Paul tells us, "Therefore, just as sin came into the world through one man, and death through sin, and so death spread to all men because all sinned" (Rom. 5:12). Adam and Eve ate the fruit and brought sin into the world, yet each of us is just as culpable. Each of us is born into sin and carries that sin with us through everything we do as we reject God and look to serve ourselves. All of us are subject to the curse pronounced in Genesis 3. That puts each of us in the same position: in the garden eating the fruit which we were commanded not to eat. Adam lives in each of us. It speaks to us of what Paul later describes in Romans 8: "For the creation was subjected to futility, not willingly, but because of him who subjected it, in hope that the creation itself will be set free from its bondage to corruption and obtain the freedom of the glory of the children of God" (vv. 20–21). The whole world groans under the weight of sin. Nowhere is that more visible than here in Genesis when, quite literally, the entire population of the world were unbelievers except for Noah and his family.

If we assert that the Flood teaches us about Baptism, then the scope of what is taking place here should be at the forefront. King David reminds us, "They have all turned aside; together they have become corrupt; there is none who does good, not even one" (Ps. 14:3). All of us have Adam's sin within us. Each of us is counted among those whose thoughts are only evil continually. Without God there is no righteousness in this fallen world. If God were today to repeat His statement—"I will blot out man whom I have created from the face of the land, man and animals and creeping things and birds of the heavens, for I am sorry that I have made them" (Gen. 6:7)—none of us would be saved from destruction without Him. God's destruction of the world is complete and total, just as total as His salvation of those He chose to save.

Baptism must then be God's action of saving those who trust Him.[2] Noah had no evidence anything would happen until the rains came.

---

2. In this sense, the work of Baptism is no different from how God initially creates faith in an individual. All aspects of justification, whether found in that initial creation of

Baptism: The Sacrament of Creation

Likewise, those who come to the font trust that God is at work to save even when nothing appears to happen immediately. However, God is truly at work. Underneath the roiling, storm-tossed waters of the Flood, God is uncreating. God is winding the clock backward to the very beginning, both in physical reality as the world is nothing more than a ball of water but also in theological reality, as God removes the taint of sin inflicted by unbelieving humanity. The days of creation rewind to a formless nothing and then, slowly, the clock starts again. The storm ceases and light shines again. The waters recede and dry land appears. Plants sprout up from the earth. Noah's ark comes to rest and, for a time, the world resembles Eden once again. It is imperfect and still marred by sin and death, but God has taught His people something very important about what true and perfect salvation will look like and how it will be accomplished.

In that mysterious way only God can know, the evil, unrighteous sinner, bearing the corruption of Adam, comes to the baptismal font and the flood waters drown him beneath the waves. The sinner's history is unraveled. His clock is rewound to a time before sin existed, and now, for him, it does not exist. He is now one who has survived the Flood because he trusted in God to save.

In God's eyes, the newly baptized is righteous. The Flood need never come for him again. God's covenant makes it clear:

> And God said, "This is the sign of the covenant that I make between Me and you and every living creature that is with you, for all future generations: I have set My bow in the cloud, and it shall be a sign of the covenant between Me and the earth. When I bring clouds over the earth and the bow is seen in the clouds, I will remember My covenant that is between Me and you and every living creature of all flesh. And the waters shall never again become a flood to destroy all flesh" (Gen. 9:12–15).

This is not a passive remembrance but an active calling to mind of the promise God made to Noah and creation. God does not see sin in one who has been baptized. He has been re-created—brought back to a state of righteousness before God. The covenant and the rainbow are not for the man, but for God—a reminder that the one who resides under the cover of the rainbow should not be washed away in a flood.[3]

---

faith or whether in Baptism, are carried out solely through the power and grace of God.

3. One could also argue from this, and, I believe rightly, that the connection between the covenant and the Flood demonstrates how rebaptizing simply does not work. The

The Flood resets the world and Baptism resets the children of Adam and Eve. Each is brought back to a state of righteousness that closely resembles what they had when they were first created. The circumstances are not quite the same, for both still stand in the eschatological context which dictates they are partial and incomplete. Both await the full and final fulfillment on the Last Day. However, for our purposes and for God's, both have accomplished their goal. For us it is as if we were still in the garden. Our righteousness is perfect and unsullied. Everything Adam and Eve had in the garden is ours now through Baptism. We enjoy eternal life and we live unafraid in the presence of Almighty God. Schmemann shares, "In the beginning, the Holy Spirit 'moved on the face of the waters,' creating the world, transforming chaos into cosmos. It is His descent, His power, His operation that now re-create the fallen world, make it again into cosmos and life."[4]

One aspect of the Flood that becomes somewhat confusing and perhaps controversial is that, in the Flood, all creation is baptized. There is not any good way to get around that notion. The text makes it quite clear the whole world is washed away and only those in the ark survive. In his commentary on Genesis 9, Luther says much the same:

> In his letter to the Corinthians (1 Cor. 10:2) Paul declares that the Israelites were baptized under Moses in the cloud and in the sea. If in this passage you look merely at conduct and words, then Pharaoh, too, was baptized, but in such a way that he perished with his men, while Israel passed through safe and unharmed. Similarly, Noah and his sons are preserved in the baptism of the Flood, while the entire remaining world outside the ark perishes because of this baptism of the Flood.[5]

Luther compares the crossing of the Red Sea to the Flood. We will deal with the Red Sea a bit later. For now, if we are assuming everyone was baptized in some sense in the Flood, then we might ask what creates the distinction between Noah and the rest of the world. Luther continues:

> The Flood is truly death and the wrath of God; nevertheless, the believers are saved in the midst of the Flood. Thus death engulfs and swallows up the entire human race; for without distinction the

---

Flood is explicitly declared to be a one-time event. The only way to argue rebaptism as legitimate is to cut out this and other threads from Baptism's theological tapestry.

4. Schmemann, *Of Water and the Spirit*, 41.
5. Luther, *Luther's Works, Vol. 2*, 152–53.

wrath of God goes over the good and the evil, over the godly and the ungodly. The Flood that Noah experienced was not different from the one that the world experienced. The Red Sea, which both Pharaoh and Israel entered, was not different. Later on, however, the difference becomes apparent in this: those who believe are preserved in the very death to which they are subjected together with the ungodly, but the ungodly perish. Noah, accordingly, is preserved because he has the ark, that is, God's promise and Word, in which he is living; but the ungodly, who do not believe the Word, are left to their fate.[6]

So, indeed, in the Flood all were baptized. All were subject to death. This is only fitting, as all who are corrupted by sin must die. The curse of Genesis 3 still holds. The distinction here is faith and trust. As we will also see elsewhere, the Old Testament themes of Baptism presume faith. Many modern denominations with a high view of the sacraments will have a corresponding shallow understanding of the work of the Spirit through the Word, particularly in the case of infants.

We see this illustrated in events such as the Flood. God tells Noah there will be a flood that will wipe out all life in the world. The only way to survive this disaster is to build an ark. Noah trusts God and takes Him at His word. Noah builds the ark and the world is then baptized. Luther responds to God's message at the beginning of Genesis 7 by saying, "Surely, great was the faith of Noah that he was able to believe these words of God. I would certainly not have believed them."[7]

More specifically about Baptism, Alexander Schmemann writes, "Faith, by being desire, makes the sacrament *possible*, for without faith it would have been 'magic'—a totally extrinsic and arbitrary act destroying man's freedom. But only God, by responding to faith, fulfills this 'possibility,' makes it truly that which faith desires: dying with Christ, rising again with Him."[8]

---

6. Luther, *Luther's Works, Vol. 2*, 153.

7. Luther, *Luther's Works, Vol. 2*, 87.

8. Schmemann, *Of Water and the Spirit*, 66–67. Italics in original. Both Luther and Schmemann describe faith as desire. For both, faith is that which desires what God freely offers and faith is completed when it receives those gifts. It should be noted that Schmemann is not arguing that man does the work of Baptism. Rather, he expresses how man's faith receives what God gives, thus allowing God's giving work to do what it intends. Faith completes the circuit. If faith had no part to play, Baptism could be forced on those without faith. Luther would also add this: "God's works are salutary and necessary for salvation, and they do not exclude but rather demand faith, for without faith one cannot

The Baptism, in Luther's sense, occurs regardless. The world is washed away. However, because Noah trusts God, he receives the fulfillment of that Baptism. Schmemann observes this in the lead up to the actual Baptism within the baptismal rite:

> Once more creation is achieved, made full and perfect. And there comes the moment when all of it "explodes" in joy and thanksgiving, bears witness to God's glory, reflects on His presence and power . . . The new creation is here, present in this baptismal font, ready for man as a gift to him of new life, light and power.[9]

Baptism is not meant to destroy but to cleanse. The rest of the world marks itself as something in need of purging, as an enemy of God, and thus could never receive what Baptism was meant to give.

Schmemann offers another thought, "It is faith that *desires* Baptism; it is faith that *knows* it to be truly dying and truly rising with Christ."[10] Faith hears God's judgment pronounced against the sinful and unbelieving world. Faith trusts that God is the only one able to save from this judgment and that He will carry about both the judgment and salvation. Faith accepts that judgment is required but also asks for undeserved mercy. Noah trusts and God is only too happy to save him from destruction. In the Flood, the world is re-created without sin, to the extent such is possible prior to the final and complete eradication of. When the floodwaters recede, all that is left is a reflection of the world's original purity.

A smaller, but nonetheless worthy, theme that corresponds to this same idea is the healing of Naaman in 2 Kings 5.[11] The simplicity of Elisha's command to Naaman brings Baptism immediately to mind. "'My father, it is a great word the prophet has spoken to you; will you not do it? Has he actually said to you, "Wash, and be clean"?' So he went down and dipped himself seven times in the Jordan, according to the word of the man of God, and his flesh was restored like the flesh of a little child, and he was clean" (2 Ki. 5:13–14). Naaman is angry at the mundaneness of the water. Such

---

grasp them" (LC IV 35). Kolb et at., *The Book of Concord*, 461.

9. Schmemann, *Of Water and the Spirit*, 52.

10. Schmemann, *Of Water and the Spirit*, 66. Italics in original.

11. Some might argue the healing of Naaman more closely corresponds to the Levitical law for the cleansing of lepers, which we will discuss a bit later. However, there is a difference in what is taking place in both instances. In the Levitical law, the lepers are already free of their disease and seek to be recognized as clean. Here, Naaman is still bearing the disease in his body. This changes the activity taking place and what we are to draw from it.

lowly water from such a lowly place could not possibly effect such a change. Yet, through the power of God's promise, a diseased man who goes into the water comes out completely clean.

What is more remarkable about this passage is how it illustrates the ongoing blessing of Baptism. Having received his healing from God and been made clean, Naaman has a brief discussion with Elisha. After Elisha refuses payment, Naaman asks for some earth where he can make sacrifices to God. He also asks for pardon for giving the appearance of idolatry as he assists the king in bowing to the false god, Rimmon.

Rather than being condemned and cast out for giving the outward appearance of continued pagan worship, Naaman is told to "Go in peace" (v. 19). The understanding is that Naaman's complicity in his king's pagan worship is as much sin as the actual pagan worship. Nevertheless, Naaman's righteousness is not in doubt. Rather than try and justify his action as unworthy of God's condemnation, he accepts it is sinful, is grieved by the fact that he feels he must do it anyway, and asks for forgiveness *before he commits the sin*.

Our baptismal grace follows this same thread. While our Baptism can be rejected, it will not fail us. We are not given carte blanche to sin however we want. Paul addresses that in Romans 6. At the same time, God's grace persists in the midst of sin and in spite of it. Every sin is a danger but that does not mean every sin immediately brings unbelief and a rejection of the Spirit. Naaman was made clean. His body is healed of the disease that outwardly displayed the effects of sin and his broken state. Now that he is healed, his body also displays the Spirit that lives within him. The Spirit is not so easily cast out.

The Creator knows all sins, past, present, and future. Christ died for all sins, regardless of when they take place. Paul also reminds us God knew us before we were even created. He knows all of our sins before we make them. Whether our sins are unintentional does not change their status as sins or affect the power of God's baptismal grace to wash them away.

For future sins to blot out our baptismal grace would mean sin has power over God and His promise of grace. If that were the case, subsequent repentance would necessitate a rebaptism, since our previous Baptism had been invalidated. Luther states this:

> Now if this covenant did not exist, and God were not so merciful as to wink at our sins, there could be no sin so small but it would condemn us. For the judgment of God can endure no sin.

> Therefore there is no greater comfort on earth than baptism. For it is through baptism that we come under the judgment of grace and mercy, which does not condemn our sins but drives them out by many trials. There is a fine sentence of St. Augustine which says, "Sin is altogether forgiven in baptism; not in such a manner that it is no longer present, but in such a manner that it is not imputed." It is as if he were to say, "Sin remains in our flesh even until death and works without ceasing. But so long as we do not give our consent to it or desire to remain in it, sin is so overruled by our baptism that it does not condemn us and is not harmful to us. Rather it is daily being more and more destroyed in us until our death."[12]

Naaman is not summarily cast out from God's presence any more than we are for any of the myriad sins we commit, knowingly or unknowingly. God's promise of grace, shared with us through our Baptism, covers them all.

We see the contrast with Elisha's servant, Gehazi, who, though he was presumably a believer as he worked together with the prophet, nevertheless sought worldly gain for God's free gift. He who was once clean now displays his sin outwardly for all to see. The baptismal cleansing that Naaman receives is rejected by Gehazi.

What is further of interest is how God uses the things of the world to re-create the world. Rather than simply calling things into being, as He does during the seven days of creation, He uses elements within creation to affect this restoration. He does not use His divine authority to command everyone except Noah and his family to die. Instead, He commands the waters under the earth to break forth and the waters above to rain down, thereby washing the world clean. Elisha could have waved his hand and declared Naaman clean. Instead Naaman is told to wash in the Jordan. God reclaims a small piece of creation to use in the restoration of that creation. God redeems that little piece of creation by giving it a new, redemptive purpose. Schmemann explains, "In the Bible, water is the symbol of *judgment* (cf. Flood), *cleansing*, i.e. forgiveness and *life*. More generally it is the 'first matter,' the root and foundation of the world. By its use in baptism, the Church prepares, as it were a new world for the new man, or rather a new relationship between the 'matter' and the man."[13]

This idea recalls Jesus' discussion with the Samaritan woman in John 4, as He explains the difference between the water from the well and the water He would give her. The water in the well is not evil or corrupt. The water

---

12. Luther, *Luther's Works*, Vol. 35, 34–35.
13. Schmemann, *Liturgy and Life*, 95. Italics in original.

is good for enabling life to continue, for without it we die. However, that is the extent of its ability. Water, by itself, can do nothing more than allow us to live another day. When God intervenes in the water, the water takes on a property it did not have on its own nor could it ever. Now God is active in and through the water to empower the water to do greater things. The water still brings life, but now it brings *even greater* life, life such as could not exist in the world otherwise. This is how eternal life must come into existence in the world. Nothing in the world has this power of itself. God must lift up this poor, fallible, earthly material and grant it a life it is not capable of producing. Seeing this happen through the waters of Baptism is then no different than seeing it happen in the lifeless body of Christ as He suddenly draws breath and lives again.

God is able to empower water to give greater life, but He is also able to empower water for greater judgment. The floods, hurricanes, and other destructive forces of weather that randomly terrorize the world hopefully drive us to trust in God as our protector, but otherwise do little to help the world. When God directs water for judgment, it is made into the ultimate cleansing tool. Water is given a purpose: to wipe out corruption and sin. The Flood does this extremely well, but Baptism has a similar purpose. Baptism judges and so it also cleanses. The Spirit gives that part of us that was created by God an ark to abide in while the sacramental waters wash the rest of us away. That permanent stain of sin is wiped clean and all that remains is that which God wishes to save.

Another instance of this idea in action is the healing at the pool at Bethesda in John 5. Here Jesus encounters an invalid who seeks to be healed in the waters that were reported to have this power when they were stirred up. Regardless of whether the water here actually had that ability or not, the power is still limited. This water might have healed the man of his infirmity, but it would not have given him eternal life.

When Jesus comes along the narrative changes. Jesus does not worry about taking the man down to the pool to be healed. Instead, He shows the power of this water as temporary. Jesus gives him something more lasting, more healing, but also the grace that leads to eternal life.

3

Baptism: The Sacrament of Vocation

PRIEST

Restoring creation to a glimmer of its original state is a mighty and powerful work. A restoration of this magnitude says how corrupt we and all creation are as a result of sin. We might be restored to the righteousness humanity had prior to sin, but that tells us little about what the purpose of that righteousness is. "What have we been re-created to do?" we might ask. Here, baptismal theology crosses over a bit into creation theology, as it must. When we understand what Adam and Eve were to do, we gain a better sense of who we are now as baptized Christians.

The very act of creating Adam is governed by God's desire to have someone who will be in His own image. It calls to mind a mirror, one that is interested in spiritual things rather than physical. In his original creation, Adam mirrored everything God did and everything God was. God loved His creation perfectly, as did Adam. God served it and tended to it. God was perfectly in sync with His creation and everything worked as it was created. Because Adam functioned perfectly, he was a perfect mirror for God's own righteousness. He reflected all of God's own virtues back to Him. He lived a sinless life, which meant not just being sinless but also fulfilling all of the responsibilities God had created him to hold.

Sin shatters that mirror. The mirror's surface is now black and broken. God looks at each of us and sees only the brokenness. A broken mirror is useless and is simply swept up and thrown away. God's wrath is precisely what awaits all sinners. We have no place or purpose in His house and so we are cast out. The duties and vocations God had given to Adam, especially those that pertained to God, could never be carried out in the manner they were intended, if he could do them at all. Imperfection cannot produce perfection, and so the broken mirror continues down through the generations to us as well. None of us reflect God as each of us seeks to become his own god.

When comparing our life today with that of Adam, Luther observes this:

> And again, the situation of Adam, as the initiator of sin, was worse than ours, if we appraise it correctly. Where we work hard, each one in his own station, Adam was compelled to exert himself in the hard work of the household, of the state, and of the church all by himself. As long as he lived, he alone held all these positions among his descendants. He supported his family, ruled it, and trained it in godliness; he was father, king, and priest. And experience teaches how each one of these positions abounds in grief and dangers.[1]

Adam held the dual roles of priest and king, the first Melchizedek. Adam oversaw all of creation. Everything that took place in the world was under his supervision. It meant he had a lot to manage, but without sin to interfere, it was a job that would never be as taxing as any duty a leader of our day might face. At the same time, Adam provided order for all the worship of God. Adam was tasked with ensuring creation acknowledged God as God and Lord over all things and praised Him accordingly. This, again, was not a difficult duty since everything was predisposed to do this anyway. Luther reflects further:

> After God has given man the administration of government and of the home, has set him up as king of the creatures, and has added the tree of life as a safeguard for preserving this physical life, He now builds him, as it were, a temple that he may worship Him and thank the God who has so kindly bestowed all these things on him. Today in our churches we have an altar for the administration of the Eucharist, and we have platforms or pulpits for teaching the people. These objects were built not only to meet a need but also to create a solemn atmosphere. But this tree of the knowledge of good and evil was Adam's church, altar, and pulpit. Here he was to yield to God the obedience he owed, give recognition to the

---

1. Luther, *Luther's Works, Vol. 1*, 213–14.

Word and will of God, give thanks to God, and call upon God for aid against temptation.[2]

Eden functions as a palace and temple where Adam and Eve serve the living God. Their failure to follow God's one prohibition meant a breakdown in both directions. Creation would no longer be ordered correctly because the king no longer cared for its well-being. Creation would no longer be able to properly serve and worship God because the priest no longer lifted up its prayers and praises to the Creator. Thankfully, the world does not completely disintegrate because God is still the Creator and still ensures His creation is able to continue.

Peter echoes the pronouncement of God as he declares the New Testament Church to be, "a spiritual house, to be a holy priesthood, to offer spiritual sacrifices acceptable to God through Jesus Christ" (1 Pet. 2:5). As sinners who carry the apostasy of Adam with us, this statement is an impossibility. Paul confirms this as he echoes King David when he says, "None is righteous, no, not one; no one understands; no one seeks for God. . . There is no fear of God before their eyes" (Rom. 3:10–11, 18). To be a priest when one neither fears nor even seeks after God is a contradiction in terms. Were we still bearing the image of God, reflecting God's righteousness back to Him, our priestly work would be self-evident. We would return to God what is His due on behalf of ourselves and those around us. But instead we are broken, and giving God anything is the furthest thing from our minds.

The priestly vocation is ultimately expressed as one of mediation through sacrifice. Nearly everything the Old Testament priests did involved sacrifices mediating the relationship between God and sinful man, whether it was animals and grain or simple prayers and praises of a grateful people. Prayerful requests were rooted in faith and trust in a loving Creator. To sacrifice something to someone else or on behalf of someone else goes against a sinner's very nature. To give something away would mean I no longer have it and, as a sinner and self-made god, I am the most important thing in creation. Schmemann says, "If the property of the king is to have power and dominion, that of the priest is to offer sacrifice, i.e. to be mediator between God and creation, the 'sanctifier' of life through its inclusion into the divine will and order."[3] To sanctify is to make holy, to cleanse those things that have been put to profane use and to take those things that are common and dedicate them to God's service.

---

2. Luther, *Luther's Works, Vol. 1*, 94–95.
3. Schmemann, *Of Water and the Spirit*, 95.

Baptism: The Sacrament of Vocation

Nevertheless, Peter's statement must also be true. God had not simply forgotten about the sins of the Israelites when He said they were "a kingdom of priests" (Ex. 19:6). There must be something else that holds these two contradictory statements together so they can both be true.

Our sinfulness precludes us from holding a priestly role or even setting foot in the presence of God without transgressing His holiness. Schmemann says, "The original sin consists in man's choice of a non-priestly relationship with God and the world."[4] Mankind seeks to be like God, just as Satan promised would happen in the Garden of Eden. Mankind's desire is to be served as a god, rather than serving anyone else.

God addresses the need for restoration, though not the manner it will be carried out, in Ezekiel 36, when He says, "I will sprinkle clean water on you, and you shall be clean from all your uncleanness, and from all your idols I will cleanse you. And I will give you a new heart, and a new spirit I will put within you. And I will remove the heart of stone from your flesh and give you a heart of flesh" (vv. 25–26). God is looking forward to restoring His people and He uses the analogy of washing to do so. It is a restoration—particularly as God speaks in terms of giving them a new heart—but it is a restoration aimed at their status as priests. Earlier in Ezekiel, God makes clear that the primary grievance is idolatry; thus the Israelites are serving as priests to the wrong gods. In order for them to truly be priests again, they must return to the one who has both made them and claimed them as His own. Only then can they resume the service they were meant to have.

However, Jesus has no such problem. The book of Hebrews repeatedly refers to Jesus as the high priest before God. In His humanity, Jesus is capable of holding this office because He lives completely free of sin. He cannot transgress the holiness of God, and He continuously offers up the prayers and thanks of all of creation to its Creator. In everything He does, Christ maintains His priestly office, maintaining the duties we have forsaken. "And every priest stands daily at his service, offering repeatedly the same sacrifices, which can never take away sins. But when Christ had offered for all time a single sacrifice for sins, He sat down at the right hand of God, waiting from that time until His enemies should be made a footstool for His feet. For by a single offering He has perfected for all time those who are being sanctified" (Heb. 10:11–14). Schmemann reflects on the priestly work of Christ:

---

4. Schmemann, *Of Water and the Spirit*, 96.

> In His Incarnation, in His self-offering to God for the salvation of the world, Christ revealed the true—the priestly—nature of man, and by the gift of His life to us—in Baptism and Chrismation—He restores us to our priest-hood: to the power of presenting our "bodies a living sacrifice, holy, acceptable unto God" (Rom. 12:1), of making our whole life a "reasonable service" (Rom. 12:1), offering sacrifice, communion.[5]

Hence, whenever we pray to the Father, we offer those prayers "in the name of Jesus Christ, Your Son, our Lord." Our prayers are offered because Christ serves as the High Priest before His Father, and we offer them through Him. It is our Baptism into the vocation of priest, our Baptism *into Christ the High Priest*, that makes this offering possible and it is on His behalf that the offering is accepted.

Christ's work does benefit us and creation. Even as enemies of God, His creatures are still brought blessings from the Father through Jesus' intercession. "For He makes His sun rise on the evil and on the good, and sends rain on the just and on the unjust" (Matt. 5:45). The death and resurrection of Christ, by itself, does nothing to change our disposition. Luther says this regarding Christ's gift through Communion:

> This treasure is conveyed and communicated to us in no other way than through the words 'given and shed for you.' Here you have both—that it is Christ's body and blood and that they are yours as a treasure and gift. Christ's body cannot be an unfruitful, useless thing that does nothing and helps no one. Yet, however great the treasure may be in itself, it must be set within the Word and offered to us through the Word, otherwise we could never know of it or seek it (LC V).[6]

We are still broken and have no interest in reflecting God's righteousness or in lifting up the prayers of creation. God must bring that gift into our lives, which He does by creating faith within that responds to the words "for you." Without this, the sacrifice of Christ is of no use to us.

Since we are unwilling and incapable of restoring ourselves to our proper place and vocation, God must do the work Himself. "For as many of you as were baptized into Christ have put on Christ" (Gal. 3:27). In these few words, Paul explains how everything is put right. The root of the problem is that we lack the image of God we were created with and no longer

---

5. Schmemann, *Of Water and the Spirit*, 97.
6. Kolb et al., *The Book of Concord*, 469.

Baptism: The Sacrament of Vocation

reflect God back to Himself, so Christ steps into the picture. As we "put on" Christ in our Baptism, God once again sees Himself when He looks at us. Now, when the Father looks at us, He sees the same righteousness and self-giving love He has Himself. We are made to look like Christ who gave Himself in service to His Father and to creation. We are perfected in Christ, so no divine judgment will find us. All of our sin is covered under the righteousness of Christ.

The re-creative work of God in Baptism is evident once more. If everything broke in the fall into sin, then the answer is to rewind time to a point prior to the entrance of sin. Schmemann offers:

> This is the *re-creation of man:* of his body, his members, his senses. Through sin man has obscured in himself the image and ineffable glory of God. He has lost his spiritual beauty; he has broken the icon. He is to be reshaped and restored. It is not with the "soul" alone that Baptism is concerned; it is with the entire man. Baptism is above all the restoration of man precisely as *wholeness,* the reconciliation of the soul and the body. "The oil of gladness": the same oil on the water and on the body of man for reconciliation with God and, in God, with the world. The same Spirit: the same life, the destruction of all false dichotomies and pseudo-spiritualities, the return to the eternal mystery of creation, ". . .and God saw that it was very good. . ." (Gen. 1:31).[7]

Baptism puts Christ over us so that, as far as God is concerned, everything we do and say is Christ working for and speaking back to His Father. We are brought into the perfect humanity of Christ and, in doing so, our own humanity is restored. In putting on Christ, we put on the priestly ephod that Adam set aside. In putting on Christ and, by faith and trust, allowing Him to do the work through us, we are once again capable of serving God and bringing the cares and concerns of the world before Him.

This priestly work is not given to any one Christian but to all. We as the church are the holy priesthood Peter describes. Luther states this:

> Baptism is an external sign or token, which so separates us from all men not baptized that we are thereby known as a people of Christ, our Leader, under whose banner of the holy cross we continually fight against sin. In this holy sacrament we must therefore pay attention to three things: the sign, the significance of it, and the faith.

---

7. Schmemann, *Of Water and the Spirit,* 53. Italics in original.

> The sign consists in this, that we are thrust into the water in the name of the Father and of the Son and of the Holy Spirit; however, we are not left there but are drawn out again. This accounts for the expression: *aus der Taufe gehoben*. The sign must thus have both its parts, the putting in and the drawing out.[8]

The whole world was baptized in the Flood, but only Noah and his family were drawn back out of the water. Luther, commenting on 1 Peter, adds:

> That water drowned everything that had life. Thus Baptism drowns everything that is carnal and natural; it makes spiritual men. But we take ship in the ark, which represents the Lord Christ, or the Christian Church, or the Gospel which Christ preaches, or the body of Christ to which we cling through faith; and we are saved, just as Noah was saved in the ark. Thus you see that the analogy summarizes what faith and the cross, life and death, are. Now where there are people who cling to Christ, there a Christian Church is sure to be. There everything that comes from Adam and is evil is drowned.[9]

The church continues this as we are baptized in the water and drawn back out, marking us as part of the community of those who have been saved by God from death in the water.

This priestly relationship is what defines the life of the church and the purpose for its existence in the world. Schmemann remarks, "[The church] is priestly in her relationship to herself, for her life is to offer herself to God, and she is priestly in her relationship to the world, for her mission is to offer the world to God and thus to sanctify it."[10] It is precisely because the church is the Body of Christ—the people declared to be a holy priesthood—that the relationship between creation and Creator is restored. Each individual joins the Body of Christ through Baptism and becomes one with Him and with all of the others throughout time who have been restored to priestly service. It carries out this duty through its worship in response to the divine *leitourgia*, the service God gives to His people as they gave in His house around His Word and sacraments.

---

8. Luther, *Luther's Works*, Vol. 35, 29–30. Italics in original. "*Aus der Taufe gehoben*" translates as "lifted up out of the baptismal water."

9. Luther, *Luther's Works*, Vol. 30, 115–16.

10. Schmemann, *Of Water and the Spirit*, 97.

Baptism: The Sacrament of Vocation

A restoration of man's priestly vocation is a restoration of man's purpose in creation. Schmemann continues:

> If in Christ man's nature itself is restored to royal priesthood and thus each human vocation, each human life can truly be "priestly," it is because He Himself had no other vocation, no other life, but to announce to men the Gospel of the Kingdom, to reveal to them the divine Truth, to bestow upon them by His self-sacrifice forgiveness of sins, salvation and the gift of new life.[11]

This fact is also found at the end in Revelation 7. The image depicts the multitude gathered around the throne of God, all wearing the white robes of Christ's righteousness and all lifting up priestly praises to God. Even in paradise, and perhaps especially so, the priestly role continues.

The priests of the temple acted as the doorkeepers to God's presence. Not that they were meant to exclude the people but that they should protect the people from harming themselves. Those who should not be in God's presence were kept from transgressing God's holiness and thus kept from sinning against it. For those whose sin precluded them from stepping into the holy place, contrition was encouraged so that absolution may be given. Thus, the priestly role was ultimately about communicating God's grace, establishing His kingdom, and thereby bringing salvation and life to His people.

In the New Testament era, the priestly work remains the same. "[Jesus] breathed on them and said to them, 'Receive the Holy Spirit. If you forgive the sins of any, they are forgiven them; if you withhold forgiveness from any, it is withheld'" (John 20:22–23). The same Spirit-filled breath that enlivened Adam on the sixth day of creation returns to the disciples and reestablishes their priestly role. We note also that this duty and responsibility was not given to any one disciple but to all, making the priestly vocation intrinsically linked to discipleship, which is joined to Baptism both through our understanding of creation and Christ's own command. We will examine this connection a bit later. For now, it is worth simply reflecting on how Christ brings the work of our re-creation full circle and gives us the ability to once again carry out the vocation we were meant to have.

---

11. Schmemann, *Of Water and the Spirit*, 98.

KING

As Luther observed earlier, Adam was given the duty to not only be priest before the world but also its king. Luther indicates that this, too, is part of nature and vocation under the image of God:

> Here [in Gen. 1:26] the rule is assigned to the most beautiful creature, who knows God and is the image of God, in whom the similitude of the divine nature shines forth through his enlightened reason, through his justice and his wisdom. Adam and Eve become the rulers of the earth, the sea, and the air.... Adam and Eve heard the words with their ears when God said: "Have dominion." Therefore the naked human being—without weapons and walls, even without any clothing, solely in his bare flesh—was given the rule over all birds, wild beasts, and fish.[12]

Adam and Eve lived as king and queen over creation, using their divinely granted authority to establish order and helping creation to flourish through their wisdom. It is the first vocation they are given, as evidenced in the first command God gives them, "And God said to them, 'Be fruitful and multiply and fill the earth and subdue it, and have dominion over the fish of the sea and over the birds of the heavens and over every living thing that moves on the earth'" (Gen. 1:28). Luther says, "After God had equipped the entire world in various ways, He also made ready the Garden of Eden, which He intended to be the dwelling place and royal headquarters of man, to whom He had assigned the rule over all the beasts."[13] Schmemann also adds, "Christianity has a cosmic dimension because the divine purpose of man, as created by God, is to be king of creation, to submit the whole cosmos to God."[14] The text of Genesis tells us Adam and Eve were not created to simply exist but to tend and care for the needs of creation. This was their responsibility and privilege. All creation eagerly obeyed the will of its human king and queen because Adam and Eve loved it with the same self-giving love God had for them. When Jesus says to the disciples in Matthew 17, "For truly, I say to you, if you have faith like a grain of mustard seed, you will say to this mountain, 'Move from here to there,' and it will move, and nothing will be impossible for you" (v. 20), He speaks of what the human

---

12. Luther, *Luther's Works, Vol. 1*, 66.
13. Luther, *Luther's Works, Vol. 1*, 101.
14. Schmemann, *Liturgy and Life*, 95.

Baptism: The Sacrament of Vocation

kings and queens of creation have the authority to do but are no longer able to carry out.

With the loss of the image of God and the corruption of sin, our reign over creation is a job we hold in name only. Not only are we completely unable to make the rest of creation follow our commands except by brute force but we have little concern for its well-being. Schmemann also offers this:

> Man was created as the king of creation: such then is the first and essential truth about man, the source and the foundation of the Christian "spirituality." To be king, to possess the gift of kingship, belongs to his very nature. He himself is from above, for it is from above that he receives the image of God and the power to make creation into that which God wants it to be and to become. He is the bearer of divine power, the *benefactor* of the earth given to him as his kingdom, for its own benefit and fulfillment.[15]

Man was created with all the faculties necessary to reign as king over creation, a king who rules not for his own benefit but for the benefit of creation.

Rejecting God in Adam's first sin, and reinforcing that rejection in every sin thereafter, each individual sets himself up as king on his own authority and allows for no Lord to hold authority over him. God rules as Servant-King, a king who holds the needs of His subjects as more important than His own. God creates Adam and Eve with the same template, but they reject the servant aspect and now can no longer meet the needs of position they are meant to hold. Schmemann offers a further thought here:

> Rejecting the power from above, ceasing to be God's anointed, he is no longer the benefactor of creation; instead of leading it to its fulfillment, he wants to benefit from it, to have and to possess it for himself. And since neither he nor creation has life in himself, his fall inaugurates the reign of death. He becomes a mortal slave of the kingdom of death.[16]

The king becomes a slave to sin and to death, ruling in a kingdom that neither obeys him nor benefits from him.

"Therefore, just as sin came into the world through one man, and death through sin, and so death spread to all men because all sinned—for sin indeed was in the world before the law was given, but sin is not counted

---

15. Schmemann, *Of Water and the Spirit*, 82. Italics in original.
16. Schmemann, *Of Water and the Spirit*, 82–83.

where there is no law. Yet death reigned from Adam to Moses, even over those whose sinning was not like the transgression of Adam, who was a type of the one who was to come" (Rom. 5:12–14). The world continues to drift away from its king as sin continues to divide. Adam is cursed to work the ground to survive. No longer can he command the earth to provide for him and creation no longer knows how best to do so. No longer is creation ordered in such a way as to sustain life. Thorns and thistles grow where food-bearing plants are meant to be. Plants grow wild and must be tamed if they will provide. Animals prowl around and devour each other instead of living together in peace. After the days of Noah animals come to fear the king and no longer listen to their king unless they are coaxed or forced to do so. We have become kings who can only rule through violence and deception.

The passage from Romans illustrates the transition, "For if, because of one man's trespass, death reigned through that one man, much more will those who receive the abundance of grace and the free gift of righteousness reign in life through the one man Jesus Christ" (Rom. 5:17). Jesus reigns as king and His reign looks very different from ours. Luther says, "Christ confessed His office before Pilate: that He is a king and that His royal office is to preach the Gospel."[17]

Paul offers more on the subject when he says this:

> For as by a man came death, by a man has come also the resurrection of the dead. For as in Adam all die, so also in Christ shall all be made alive. But each in his own order: Christ the first fruits, then at his coming those who belong to Christ. Then comes the end, when he delivers the kingdom to God the Father after destroying every rule and every authority and power. For he must reign until he has put all his enemies under his feet. The last enemy to be destroyed is death (1 Cor. 15:21–26).

Jesus reigns as King as well, but His reign undoes what Adam's did. As God resets creation, a perfect man again reigns over creation and creation responds to Him as it was intended. Where the first perfect man refused his duty and brought death into the world, the second perfect man rules as He was intended and brings life. Creation orders itself around Him as everything that is broken and corrupted is made right once more.

Schmemann reflects on Christ's human nature:

---

17. Luther, *Luther's Works*, Vol. 69, 214.

Baptism: The Sacrament of Vocation

> In Christ, the Savior and the Redeemer of the World, man is restored to his essential nature—and this means that he is made a king again. We often forget that Christ's title as King—the title which He affirms when He makes His triumphant entrance into Jerusalem and is greeted as "the King that comes in the name of the Lord," the title which He accepts when He stands before Pilate: "thou sayest that I am a king" (John 18:37)—is His human, and not only divine, title. He is the King, and He manifests Himself as King because He is the New Adam, the Perfect Man—because He restores in Himself human nature in its ineffable glory and power.[18]

The baptized Christian who has put on Christ is seated once again on the throne to rule over creation, serving as king or queen under the King of kings. The Christian who is restored to his kingly vocation now seeks to reorder creation. The king cares for his subjects and works to reorder creation in the manner it was created. Creation's disorder comes about because of the failure of its ruler, so helping to order and organize creation enables it to work the way it was intended and eases the suffering of the world and all who dwell in it.

This means man's vocation as king is good. The failure of creation to respond lies with us. Schmemann adds this:

> It is indeed the first fruit in us of restored *kingship* that we not only can, but spiritually speaking must, while in this wicked world, *rejoice* in its essential goodness and make this joy, this gratitude, this knowledge of creation's goodness the very foundation of our own life; that behind all deviations, all "brokenness," all evil we can *detect* the essential nature and vocation of man and all that exists and that was given to man as his kingdom.[19]

In our day, rulers, kings, and politicians all have a reputation for self-serving greed and power-mongering. It is often assumed that any politician who makes it into office is out for his or her own interests first and foremost. Adam was created to be a servant to his subjects—to care for their needs first and to ensure the joy and prosperity of those under him.

Jesus reorients our idea of rulership. He tells His disciples, "The kings of the Gentiles exercise lordship over them, and those in authority over them are called benefactors. But not so with you. Rather, let the greatest among you become as the youngest, and the leader as one who serves. For who is

---

18. Schmemann, *Of Water and the Spirit*, 83.
19. Schmemann, *Of Water and the Spirit*, 85. Italics in original.

the greater, one who reclines at table or one who serves? Is it not the one who reclines at table? But I am among you as the one who serves" (Luke 22:25–27). He washes their feet, He goes to the cross, sacrificing Himself for the benefit of those under Him, all the while maintaining His authority to reign as king and preaching the good news of His kingdom. As Luther says of the Second Article, "As his own possession he has taken us under his protection and shelter, in order that he may rule us by his righteousness, wisdom, power, life, and blessedness" (LC II).[20] He also says in his explanation of the Second Petition of the Lord's Prayer, "What is the kingdom of God? Answer: Simply what we heard above in the Creed, namely, that God sent his Son, Christ our Lord, into the world to redeem and deliver us from the power of the devil, to bring us to himself, and to rule us as a king of righteousness, life, and salvation against sin, death, and an evil conscience" (LC III).[21]

The world praises the king who rides into Jerusalem, thinking He will do what they want. They scorn Him a short while later when it becomes clear He is not the king they think He is. The corrupted and disordered world cannot comprehend what it is meant to look like on its own. Christ upends the world's understanding of rule, reorienting it from domination to service. Jesus is the King who is due all honor and glory. He cannot be forced to do anything. It is through His own choice that He wraps a towel around His waist and washes feet or touches lepers. He is the crucified King who offers the greatest act of service possible. "For this reason the Father loves Me, because I lay down My life that I may take it up again. No one takes it from Me, but I lay it down of My own accord. I have authority to lay it down, and I have authority to take it up again" (John 10:17–18). He gives His life to teach us what it means to be king but also to give us the ability to begin carrying out that reign in the broken world in which we currently live.

The baptized Christian becomes a king once more, a ruler of creation in the position and vocation he was created to hold. A re-created creation, one that has been purged of self-service and reordered to serve others, will again give the honor due to its human kings. Each individual Christian is a king or a queen, charged with caring for the world and bringing order so that life will flourish and beauty will fill the earth. The command of God in Genesis 1 still stands. As kings and queens resume their duties, order is restored and creation learns again how it is meant to grow and flourish.

20. Kolb et al., *The Book of Concord*, 434.
21. Kolb et al., *The Book of Concord*, 446.

Baptism: The Sacrament of Vocation

Though we hold the vocation of king in truth, even now through our Baptism, creation does not respond as it ought. Like Christ, we rule a kingdom that is not of the here and now. "My kingdom is not of this world. If My kingdom were of this world, My servants would have been fighting, that I might not be delivered over to the Jews. But My kingdom is not from the world . . . You say that I am a king. For this purpose I was born and for this purpose I have come into the world—to bear witness to the truth" (John 18:36–37). The king who rode into Jerusalem on Palm Sunday was rejected because those welcoming Him expected the kingdom to be established according to their demands. Such a kingdom could never last.

In the beginning of creation, king and kingdom lived together in perfect unity. Each person, creature, and plant had its role and carried out its duties with no thought to do anything else. Everything worked as it was meant to. When the first king subverted his rule, all his subjects suffered as well. Christ works to restore everything to the perfection it was always intended to have. However, He cannot restore creation without first restoring the kings and queens to rule it. Otherwise, the whole avalanche of corruption would come rolling down on the innocent world once more. No, Christ first restores the king so he will be ready for when Christ restores creation.

We are restored to a renewed state of righteousness as we put on Christ in our Baptism, but the kingdom we are to co-rule is one that does not fully exist yet. Speaking again of Jesus' conversation with Pilate in John 18, Luther explains further, "[Jesus] says: "Pilate, everything I have proclaimed is the pure truth; it is for this that I was born. It is My royal office to preach the truth."[22] Jesus' reign is primarily to proclaim the truth; the truth that this world can never be made into a utopia. Lasting peace will never be found here. The world is broken. Death touches everything here and only in the Baptism by fire that Christ Himself will bring can it be remade in the original state we have been given through our Baptism in water. Schmemann explains further:

> It is the mystery of the Cross, and that mystery alone, that *holds together* the two affirmations which on the level of human reasoning cannot be reconciled: the one about man and his royal calling in God's creation, and the one about the Kingdom "not of this world." . . . By being, first of all, the true and the ultimate revelation of *this world* as the fallen world, whose fall, whose "wickedness" consists

---

22. Luther, *Luther's Works*, Vol. 69, 214.

in the rejection by it of God and of His Kingship and thus of the true life given to it in creation.[23]

A creation that sacrifices its own king to serve its own selfishness can never be fixed. It must be remade, re-created. The cross of Christ becomes the bridge, connecting this broken kingdom that suffers from our disordered reign with that of the kingdom yet to come.

That means we are ultimately people who await the creation and kingdom we are meant to rule. Schmemann explains:

> [The Cross] inaugurates the Kingdom of God by revealing it to be not "another world," another creation "replacing" this one, but the same creation, though liberated from the "Prince of this world," restored to its true nature and to its ultimate destiny—when "God shall be all in all" (1 Cor. 15:28).[24]

We await the Baptism Christ brings to creation, washing all evils away as we saw in the world's first baptism, the Flood. We look forward to the time when we can step out into a creation that has been washed clean, just as Noah did.

PROPHET

The last of those vocations to which we have been restored is that of the prophet. The tendency for Christians is to think of prophecy as merely "telling the future." However, this would be narrowing prophecy too much and risks turning a prophet into simply a soothsayer. God tells Moses:

> I will raise up for them a prophet like you from among their brothers. And I will put My words in His mouth, and He shall speak to them all that I command Him. . . . And if you say in your heart, "How may we know the word that the Lord has not spoken?"— when a prophet speaks in the name of the Lord, if the word does not come to pass or come true, that is a word that the Lord has not spoken; the prophet has spoken it presumptuously. You need not be afraid of him. (Deut. 18:18, 21–22)

Prophets often did tell the future, but they would also share any other message God wanted conveyed. A prophet was someone God spoke to and who carried His message. Luther says of this passage, "This also clearly

---

23. Schmemann, *Of Water and the Spirit*, 87. Italics in original.
24. Schmemann, *Of Water and the Spirit*, 88.

proves that the Prophet will teach something different. These are words which He has not yet put into the mouth of Moses or commanded; but He promises that He will do so in the future."[25] Moses was indicating one would come who would continue to speak the word of God to the people, continuing the prophetic role while also expressing the importance of that role. Schmemann adds, "The prophet is the one who hears God and therefore can convey God's will to the world, the one who 'reads' all events, all 'situations' with God's eyes and therefore can refer all that is human and temporal to that which is divine and eternal—the one, in other words, for whom the world is transparent to God."[26]

Adam had this role naturally when he lived in the image of God, because it was part of that very nature to know God and His will and to pass along what had been spoken to him. Luther comments this on Genesis 3: "Before the desire to eat of the fruit arose in Eve, she lost the Word which God spoke to Adam. If she had adhered to this Word, she would have continued in the fear and faith of God. Where the opposite happens and the Word is lost, there is contempt of God and obedience to the devil."[27] With that connection to God's Word lost, everything that follows is inevitable: the fear, the blaming, the disordering of the world, and the loss of Paradise. Everything in creation moves according to God's command. Now, even if Adam and Eve had held on to their vocations as king and queen and desired to carry out their duty, they had no way of doing so. Like a broken radio that can no longer receive a signal, God was speaking but they were not listening. Disorder would still have crept into creation and eventually have brought it all crashing down because Adam and Eve no longer had the knowledge or ability necessary to maintain it.

Luther describes the Prophet who will follow Moses as having God's words put into His mouth. The imagery is almost that of a puppet who cannot function on its own but must have someone acting for it. Prior to sin, Adam would have actively sought out God's word and would have eagerly shared it with the world. Now he does neither.

The connection to Christ as the new prophet is clear. One was meant to lead to the other. Luther explains:

> This is the chief passage in this whole book and a clearly expressed prophecy of Christ as the new Teacher. Hence the apostles also

---

25. Luther, *Luther's Works, Vol. 9*, 182.
26. Schmemann, *Of Water and the Spirit*, 100.
27. Luther, *Luther's Works, Vol. 1*, 158.

courageously adduce this passage (Acts 3:22–23; Acts 7:37). Appropriately, Moses places it here at the end, after he has finished his discourses concerning the priesthood, the kingdom, the government, and the whole worship of God. It is his purpose to show that in the future there will be another priesthood, another kingdom, another worship of God, and another word, by which all of Moses will be set aside. Here Moses clearly describes his own end, and he yields his mastery to the Prophet who is to come.[28]

Where Adam has failed, Christ, in His humanity, will follow through. "For I have not spoken on My own authority, but the Father who sent Me has Himself given Me a commandment—what to say and what to speak. And I know that His commandment is eternal life. What I say, therefore, I say as the Father has told Me" (John 12:49–50). Jesus' human nature speaks what has been given by God.

Luther describes this speaking role further when he looks again at Jesus' conversation with Pilate: "Moses' voice is his teaching about how we are to do good works. But Christ teaches something higher, namely, how and by what means we are saved."[29] Through the presence of Christ in us, through us, and around us, we are recipients of the truth, of God's Word for the world.

Jesus speaks prophetically throughout His earthly ministry. "Look at the fig tree, and all the trees. As soon as they come out in leaf, you see for yourselves and know that the summer is already near. So also, when you see these things taking place, you know that the kingdom of God is near" (Luke 21:29–31). Here Jesus speaks of the future. He speaks about the kingdom of God and tells us the kingdom resides in the future. This is far from the only place Jesus speaks about the kingdom of God, but here we learn an important detail about God's kingdom. Because the kingdom has yet to come, the future is simply that which God has declared but has yet to come to pass.

The truth Jesus shares is God's pronouncement of judgment against sin and salvation through Christ. God has declared His will on these matters, which makes any message relating to them prophetic. Schmemann says:

> The gift of prophecy is not above and outside of true human nature restored by Christ, but rather the essential, the *vertical* dimension of all its components, of all human gifts and vocations. In Christ

---

28. Luther, *Luther's Works*, Vol. 9, 176.
29. Luther, *Luther's Works*, Vol. 69, 214.

the essential knowledge has been given to us: the *knowledge of Truth*—about God and man, about the world and its ultimate destiny. And it is this Truth that makes us truly *free*, capable of discernment and understanding, that endows us with the power to be—in all conditions and situations, in all professions and vocations, in the use of all of our human gifts—always and everywhere *witnesses to Christ*, Who is the ultimate Meaning, Content and End of all that we are, of all that we do.[30]

Through the work of the Holy Spirit, Christ is revealed and given to us. Paul reminds us, "We were buried therefore with Him by baptism into death, in order that, just as Christ was raised from the dead by the glory of the Father, we too might walk in newness of life" (Rom. 6:4). We are not just baptized to know Christ and learn about salvation. We are baptized into Christ's *life*; everything He is and everything He does. Christ prophetically proclaims the kingdom of God. He tells the people what it looks like and what happens there. He tells people how they can become a part of it. He also tells them it is something to look forward to because it has not fully arrived yet. This becomes our life too.

On the surface, not everything a prophet said was about the future. But, in His ministry, Christ is telling us it all truly was about the future. Every word God gave to the prophets to speak is something that is coming to fruition through Christ in His kingdom, the *kingdom to come.*

Our prophetic role is no different from that of those who have gone before. We stand in the line of prophets down through the ages and proclaim to the world what is yet to come. All the prophecies and promises of God are moving inexorably toward their conclusion. The promised Savior and King has come, but He will also return. We proclaim the truth of the future as we speak Christ's own words to an unbelieving world and so fulfill our own prophetic vocation.

Looking at all these vocations that are part and parcel of the image of God gives us a true sense of how far we have fallen on account of sin. Righteousness before God is not merely a matter of doing good works but of resuming an entire way of life we have lost. The magnitude of the responsibilities we are meant to bear is impossible for our sin-darkened bodies and minds to handle. Hebrews 7 and 8 describes Jesus as the true and great High Priest. He is the "guarantor of a better covenant" (7:22), a referent to the baptismal promise made to us which is only possible because He is able

---

30. Schmemann, *Of Water and the Spirit,* 103. Italics in original.

to function as a priest before the Father. He alone "always lives to make intercession for them" (7:25).

Yet, we were intended to carry out this role and our failure to do so is ever before us—not just as priests but kings and prophets as well. This is why we consider the grace given in Baptism and see the sanctifying effect that it also offers—as a resumption of the image of God we were created to have. This is why Hebrews 12:23-24 describes among the collected saints "the spirits of the righteous made perfect." It is not that they were perfect, but that they have been *made* perfect through this restorative washing, shared with us by the authority of "Jesus, the mediator of a new covenant." Through His mediation and intercession, we are made like Him, He who is the very image of His Father in heaven, and are thus restored to what we were created to be.

We find this unfolding in the short story of Jonah the prophet. At the beginning of the story, Jonah is told by God to go to Nineveh and prophesy God's coming judgment against them. God, in His mercy, gives Nineveh another chance. He sends His messenger to call attention to their sin, a primary function of the prophetic vocation. Like all of God's prophets before and since, Jonah does not declare himself a prophet. God places him into that vocation. "Now the word of the Lord came to Jonah the son of Amittai, saying..." (Jonah 1:1).

Jonah displays the effects of sin on the heart as he runs, quite literally, away from God. Though he had been placed in the prophetic role, he had no interest in carrying it out. Nevertheless, the job was his and the work must be completed. When Jonah finally gives up and realizes he cannot escape "the Lord, the God of heaven, who made the sea and the dry land" (Jonah 1:9), he throws himself overboard.

Like the Flood, Jonah's time in the belly of the fish outwardly looks like it might connect to our understanding of Baptism and, thankfully, Jesus Himself makes this connection clearer. Jesus declares to the scribes and Pharisees, "An evil and adulterous generation seeks for a sign, but no sign will be given to it except the sign of the prophet Jonah. For just as Jonah was three days and three nights in the belly of the great fish, so will the Son of Man be three days and three nights in the heart of the earth" (Matt. 12:39-40). Now we see the salvation of Jonah by the fish relates directly to Jesus' own death and resurrection and thus to Baptism's role in bringing death to sin and new life to the believer.

Baptism: The Sacrament of Vocation

With this in mind, we start bringing the larger body of baptismal theology to bear and we find an often-overlooked thread to the story of Jonah. Yes, salvation came to Nineveh as they heard God's judgment and repented in sackcloth and ashes. Yes, Jonah, like Noah before him, was "baptized" in the water and then drawn out again, not to die like others do who are cast into the deeps. However, Nineveh's salvation comes as a direct result of Jonah's preaching. Nineveh is saved because *Jonah was restored to his prophetic office through his Baptism.* Luther shares a thought here as well as he discusses Jonah 3:1–2:

> This is written that we may guard against undertaking anything without God's word and command. The first command of God had been nullified by Jonah's disobedience. Thus if God had not repeated His order, Jonah would not have known whether or not he was still to execute it. He might have shared the experience of the children of Israel (Num. 14:1 f.; Deut. 1:41 f.), who at first refused to comply with God's command to fight and later presumed to do this on their own responsibility and then suffered defeat because of their presumption. It is utterly futile and wrong for man to undertake a project of his own choosing and will without God's command and word. Moreover, this second commission contains the added command to preach what God tells him. Thus both the office and the Word employed in the office must be comprehended in the divine command.[31]

God, in His omnipotence, could have thundered from on high and declared His judgment against Nineveh all on His own. Instead, He works salvation in the life of Jonah, restoring him to the vocation and office he was always meant to fill. By following through on the job he has been given, the natural order of God's creation works as it was meant to function. Jonah begins to live out a life in the image of God. His restoration is not perfect, as evidenced by his ongoing frustration with God in chapter 4, and he will need to continue learning what it means to be a prophet throughout his life. Still, for both Jonah and the people of Nineveh, death has turned to life through God's baptismal work.

---

31. Luther, *Luther's Works, Vol. 19*, 83.

4

Baptism: The Sacrament of Eternity

WHEN WE CONSIDER PAUL'S words that we are baptized into Christ's death and subsequent resurrection, the conclusion that is usually drawn is that we now have eternal life because Christ's resurrection is ours as well. This conclusion is true, so far as it goes. However, Paul doesn't say we are given Christ's resurrection. As I briefly described earlier, our Baptism brings us newness of life through Christ Jesus. The very manner in which Christ now lives is qualitatively different. Everything Jesus does now, post-resurrection, is marked by that resurrection and everything that goes with it.

What evils could afflict Jesus before His resurrection are now powerless. Mortal pain and death are behind Him. His life is of one who has gone beyond death to a more glorious life. Likewise, our Baptism does much more than give us a life that goes on and on forever. It gives us a *new* life, one that is qualitatively different from the life we live now. Schmemann offers this:

> Thus the grace of Baptism was this very event; a man dying and rising again "in the likeness" and "after the pattern" of Christ's Death and Resurrection; it was the gift to him not of "something" resulting from these events, but of that unique and totally new possibility: truly to die with Christ, truly to rise again with Him so that he may "walk in the newness of life."[1]

Luther offers a few points of his own: "Wherefore St. Paul, in Romans 6[:4], says, 'We were buried with Christ by baptism into

---

1. Schmemann, *Of Water and the Spirit*, 58.

death.' The sooner a person dies after baptism, the sooner is his baptism completed."[2]

Luther notes how the two go together: death and Baptism. Death ends up completing in our mortal bodies what has already been done for us spiritually: a purification from sin inside and out. Where our souls have been re-created in the manner and likeness of what man had before sin, now our bodies follow suit. Luther says, "It is as if the sponsors, when they lift the child up out of baptism, were to say, 'Lo, your sins are now drowned, and we receive you in God's name into an eternal life of innocence.'"[3]

That means, unlike how we tend to superficially think about it, Baptism is a cleansing of both *soul and body*. That one aspect of this cleansing occurs later than the other does not change the fact that they are both part of the same act. The Baptism of Noah's Flood was anything but brief, yet his salvation was assured the moment the door closed on the ark.

Still, the creation we have been restored to is not completely identical to that of Genesis 1 and 2. Adam and Eve started out in a state of perfection. For them, there existed two possibilities: they could continue in the state of righteousness with which they had been created, or they could opt to disobey God and bring death into the world. With the Fall, the option to continue in righteousness no longer existed. God Himself had to re-create that option. This is what the death and resurrection of Christ, and our subsequent Baptism into that death and resurrection, brings about. For us, everything is reversed. Continuing on means existing in a world of corruption and death. Baptism into Christ puts us on a new track away from our original destination and brings about a life where death has no power. Baptized into Christ's life, death is simply no longer possible.[4] That makes the new creation we are entering immeasurably better than the original, even though the two look similar on the surface.

This new creation intersects the history of this world the moment the stone is rolled back from Christ's empty tomb. This is the moment a life beyond death first entered the world. As Schmemann said earlier, Christ

---

2. Luther, *Luther's Works, Vol. 35*, 31.
3. Luther, *Luther's Works, Vol. 35*, 31.
4. This sort of mentality can sometimes be construed as "once saved, always saved." However, Luther's point regarding Baptism must be kept in mind. The death of our mortal bodies is the completion of Baptism. The full effects of Baptism can only be viewed eschatologically. Were someone to be baptized and reject that Baptism prior to death, it would be akin to Noah jumping overboard twenty days into the storm. He would perish just as surely as everyone else outside the ark.

describes His kingdom as a "kingdom to come." This is seen immediately at His own resurrection. That there is a place where life exists without death we cannot doubt. Christ Himself demonstrates this life. But we live in a time of promise and not of fulfillment.

Nevertheless, that re-creation has already begun. It is only right and proper that Christ's resurrection and the inauguration of that new creation happen not within the seven days of creation but on the eighth day, a day outside of the old creation. While our Baptism into Christ has restored our righteousness and spiritually brought us to the state we had at creation, our circumstances now are very different from what Adam experienced. Schmemann explains further:

> Yet this "good" world, which the Jew blesses on the seventh day, is at the same time the world of sin and revolt against God, and its time is the time of man's exile and alienation from God. And, therefore, the seventh day points beyond itself toward a new Lord's Day—the day of salvation and redemption, of God's triumph over His enemies. In the late Jewish apocalyptic writings there emerges the idea of a new day which is both the *eighth*—because it is beyond the frustrations and limitation of "seven," the time of *this world*—and the *first*, because with it begins the new time, that of the Kingdom.[5]

In his day, King Solomon laments "there is nothing new under the sun" (Eccl. 1:9). However, now there exists something truly new. God has brought into being life that will never again be subject to death. This resembles the old creation in many ways, but now something has come into the world which has never been seen before. This new creation grows out of the old creation but is distinct from it. An eighth day of creation communicates that what Christ has brought into being cannot be considered in the same category as God's original seven-day work of creation.

This concept of the eighth day crops up in several places within Scripture, all of which have threads drawing the distinct ideas of Baptism and re-creation more tightly together. The first place we see this concept appear in Scripture is with the covenant God establishes with Abraham. Genesis 17 shares the conversation God has with Abraham, establishing that Abraham will indeed be the father of many nations. Abraham had already been blessed by God, but now that blessing and promise was bound to him in a more concrete fashion. The covenant is one of new life, as it is through the

---

5. Schmemann, *For the Life of the World*, 50–51. Italics in original.

children of Abraham that Christ comes into the world and through Christ that all creation is redeemed. The outward circumcision becomes a sign for what has already taken place inwardly and what will eventually be given outwardly.[6]

As with salvation and the other effects of Baptism, the power of the rite comes not from the actual doing of the rite but from the promise attached to it. Luther attacks those who think circumcision made Abraham righteous, "But for the descendants of Abraham circumcision was a symbol that they were the heirs of the promise which had been given to Abraham before he was circumcised."[7] Just as circumcision marked one as being one of God's chosen people and treasured possessions, as one among whom the Savior would be born, Baptism likewise marks you as one of God's chosen and one for whom the Savior will return. In both cases, the rite signifies a relationship to God that establishes who you are in the present but has you looking forward to the fulfillment to come. Luther says a bit more about the connection between circumcision and Baptism:

> Circumcision was only for Abraham and the Jews, but baptism is for all nations, large and small, young and old. Circumcision doesn't save, but it was attached to the future Christ. Even so, the promise which is added makes baptism. Abraham had the Word along with circumcision. Hence baptism is no more than water, but the water has been surrounded by the Word. Baptism offers as much as circumcision used to. It was proper for Abraham to say, "I have been circumcised, and in that circumcision Christ was promised to me." The promise does it. In the New Testament the promise is, "I shall be your God," and it is on this promise

---

6. One could infer from God's wording that circumcision is meant to be a dedication of the person to God. While the outward aspect of circumcision does allow for this, circumcision is not primarily meant to be a dedication. The previous baptismal covenant found after the Flood describes the rainbow as a sign meant for God and not for man. God looks down and remembers He is not to wipe away humanity. In this case we again find God establishing the covenant. This is not an agreement between equals but a promise given from one party to the other. Thus, circumcision is not man's effort to give himself to God but rather man's acceptance of the blessings God has promised. A better way to think of it is that it is not man's work that earns God's blessings but rather the following of God's commands that makes man capable of receiving what God offers. After the Fall, Adam and Eve were barred from the tree of life, and the eternal life it gave, on account of sin. We sinners are not capable of holding eternal life even as God offers it. We must be re-created through Baptism to that point prior to the Fall so that we can even use what God freely gives.

7. Luther, *Luther's Works*, Vol. 3, 87.

> that you should be baptized. In itself circumcision was nothing. So it doesn't help the Turks when they are circumcised because the promise is lost. If the promise were absent I would thumb my nose at the water. Accordingly the patriarchs received the promise, "I will be your God," and then they were circumcised. However, there is this difference between circumcision and baptism, namely, that circumcision was performed before Christ in anticipation of the very grace which is in baptism, while baptism is observed after Christ on the strength of the grace which he has secured. The grace is the same, and the only difference is between the past and future tense. However, both look to the last judgment when all will be revealed.[8]

Both circumcision and Baptism are made effective through the promise of God. Both bind the recipient to God and thus also to everything God would be doing for him from that point forward.

The eighth day, made concrete in Christ, is already visible in circumcision. On the eighth day of life, the newborn Israelite boys are circumcised and given something they had lost: a relationship with the Creator. Luther continues, "In almost the same way circumcision is a sacrament for the descendants of Abraham because, since they have the promise, they are made righteous by believing this promise and making use of the sacrament in faith."[9] The sin of the Fall had robbed mankind of this relationship, but now it was given back to them and life begins to return to what it was meant to be. They are joined to the "kingdom of priests and a holy nation" (Ex. 19:6) that God had consecrated them to be and the baptismal restoration of their vocation is begun.[10]

Just as circumcision never needs to be done again, so too does Baptism effect an everlasting change in its recipient. The eighth day becomes bound to the resurrection of Christ, eternally bound to life beyond death. Luther agrees as he writes, "This has been thought out wisely, learnedly, and piously, namely, that the eighth day is the eternal day. For the rising Christ

---

8. Luther, *Luther's Works*, Vol. 54, 55.
9. Luther, *Luther's Works*, Vol. 3, 87.
10. Luther also makes the point that circumcision implies Baptism was only meant to be done once. "Circumcision, however, took place only once during an entire lifetime; nor could it be repeated, just as in the New Testament it is sufficient to be baptized in the name of Jesus only once, and it is sinful to repeat Baptism."
Luther, *Luther's Works*, Vol. 3, 87.

is no longer subject to days, months, weeks, or any number of days; He is in a new and eternal life."[11]

This restoration of vocation continues in Leviticus 8. Here we find Aaron and his sons being consecrated for their role as priests. This is where the rite of consecration detailed in Exodus 29 is finally carried out in the midst of the people. Already we see a connection to the restoration of our priestly vocation. Aaron and his sons are consecrated, set aside by God for the holy role and duty of standing in His presence on behalf of the people. Our consecration for the role of priest through Holy Baptism is prefigured here.

Everything God commands for the ordination of Aaron and his sons is aimed at demonstrating to both the five to be ordained and to the nation of Israel what it means to be a priestly mediator and intercessor. God is also making a very visible confirmation that He has approved them for this role. Aaron is anointed with holy oil. He wears the priestly garments that mark his position, including the breastpiece which represents each of the twelve tribes. Sacrifices are offered on his behalf, prefiguring the later sacrifice of Christ. Aaron and his sons remain in the tabernacle seven days for their ordination.

Already, God is doing much to establish Aaron and his sons in their position. However, the entire work finally comes to fruition not on the seventh day, as one might expect, but on the eighth. The eighth day of the process is when Aaron finally begins his work and the redemptive activity he is to facilitate can commence. Leviticus 9 continues the event, where Aaron offers further sacrifices. The sacrifices Aaron offers are not for himself or his sons but for the people. He pours the blood out at the side of the altar, as commanded, and burns the appropriate pieces of the sacrifices on the altar, and God accepts the sacrifices. It is then that Aaron conveys the blessing of God to the people and the glory of the Lord is revealed to the assembled people.

It is through this eight-day process that Aaron is restored to what all men were meant to be. God chooses him and establishes him in the public role of priest and, once established, God and creation are able to once again communicate as they were intended. In an active and public sense, these priests are doing what Adam and all mankind were meant to do all along. The glory of the Lord appears as confirmation of the relationship He has now with His people. Adam and Eve were able to converse with God freely,

---

11. Luther, *Luther's Works, Vol. 3*, 141.

sharing their thoughts and lifting up the needs of the world around them. Now the people of Israel have that again through their priestly intercessors.

As discussed above, our priestly vocation is restored through our Baptism into Christ. Here that restoration is seen explicitly as God is at work re-creating what His people once had. Creation needs a priest to make sure its needs are met and also to tell how God is at work to meet those needs. Here on the eighth day, the world sees God publicly declare a priest has reentered the service he was meant to have.

A perhaps even more telling example of the restoration found on the eighth day is described in Leviticus 14. Here we find God giving an object lesson to the Israelites. To be unclean means to be cut off from the presence of God. It means being cut off from those God calls His treasured possession. In the case of lepers, the disease was not a sentence of condemnation, but the Israelites were meant to see this and understand the significance of being unclean and how it relates to God and to the ability to be in His presence.

In this case, the leprous person seeks to be marked as clean from his ailment. He takes various items to offer a sacrifice whereby he is sprinkled seven times with the blood of one bird while a second bird symbolically takes the uncleanness away. After this he shaves off all his hair and bathes. He comes in the camp, but stays outside his tent seven days, then repeats the shaving and washing. At this point, on the eighth day, he brings a sacrifice to the priest who offers it on his behalf and finally pronounces him clean.

As in Aaron's ordination, seven days are delineated, followed by the completion of the work on day eight. The first seven days demonstrate a resetting, a re-creation of the man. The leprous, unclean man who finds his disease has gone away comes to the priest and seeks to be made clean.[12] After performing the sacrifice of the bird, the man shaves off all his hair. The man who once bore in his body the outward evidence of sin now shaves himself completely bald. He now resembles the lifeless clay form of the first man before God breathed life into him. The unclean man is physically returned to the sixth day of creation. He washes himself so he is fresh and new. He lives like this for seven days as he relives God's creative work before going through the shaving and washing process one more time.

He comes before the priest as a renewed man, re-created. The seven days of waiting were important, but the eighth day of the process is when

---

12. This is another place that implies faith exists prior to Baptism. The leprous person only seeks out the priest when his disease is already healed; otherwise, he would simply be turned away. This cleansing rite is a confirmation of what has already taken place.

everything comes together. Here, when he is pronounced clean, the man receives back everything the disease had taken from him. He is able to live among the people again. His family and friends are restored to him. His livelihood is his once more. More importantly, he receives back what Adam and Eve had in the garden: the ability to worship God in person. Now he is welcome again in the holy places and can enter without fear of transgressing. He is made fresh and new and now can also resume the priestly vocation he had.[13] While he was diseased, he had no ability to intercede on behalf of creation because he had no access to God. Now that vocation is restored. The man can come before God both to speak on behalf of the world and to convey God's blessings to that world.

Further weight is brought to bear from the unceasing fountain of baptismal theology that is the Flood. Genesis 7:10 tells us, "And after seven days the waters of the flood came upon the earth." Noah had trusted God and the time was now at hand for the rain to come. Seven days pass as Noah makes his final preparations. It is then, on the eighth day of counting, that Noah is safely shut into the ark by God and the coming judgment against sin is already passing him by. The re-creating process has officially begun, and Noah and his family alone will be there to see it.

God's restorative work in cleansing lepers tells us much about what happens when we approach the font to be baptized. The humble sinner repents and comes to the waters to receive God's grace and now is forgiven. The stain of sin has been washed clean by the blood of the sacrifice. Now the humble and forgiven believer seeks to take his place once more in the presence of God. For this to happen, God must pronounce the believer clean. Baptism becomes the public affirmation by God that the believer is indeed free of the stain of sin.[14]

When the temple curtain tears in two from top to bottom at Christ's crucifixion, the sign is that it is no longer necessary for us to have a priest offer sacrifices for us to enter into God's presence. However, that is only

---

13. Since the whole nation of Israel was meant to be priests, Aaron and his sons are the priests to the priests. It is Aaron's full-time job to carry out his priestly duties on behalf of the nation so the nation, in turn, can be priests before the rest of the world.

14. This also shows that the direction of action in Baptism continues to be consistent. Aside from the simple following of directions, the person seeking to be clean has little part to play in the proceedings. He had no power to make the disease leave him, nor can he pronounce himself clean. All the important work is carried out either by God or His priestly representative. Thus, this passage reinforces the idea that Baptism is not primarily an act carried out by the Christian but rather by God.

true because we are *in Christ*. It is His priestly evaluation that pronounces us clean. It is His priestly robe that covers us and gives us free passage.

The eighth day is established within the history of our world—a world that continues to be bound to a week with only seven days, with the opening of the tomb. Like the light that God called into existence on the first day, Christ, "the light [that] shines in the darkness" (John 1:5), enters again into the darkness of this world. He brings His own pure and unblemished life and light into the world that all men might live as He now does. Since we are baptized into Christ, we are likewise baptized into a new world. Those who live without Christ are trapped in an endless cycle of time where each day and each week follows the last in a fixed progression. The week repeats itself over and over into the dark and winding eternity. As Christ shatters the bonds of death, He simultaneously breaks the Sabbath cycle that causes the week to repeat itself once again.

The Christian who is baptized into His death and resurrection follows Him through this fissure at the end of the week into a truly *new* day. This day marks the beginning of eternity. Never again will the Christian need to relive the creation of the world. He has been truly re-created. He is restored to that righteousness and life he was meant to have and he will never lose it again. The Christian is truly *made new* and only has an eternal life to live in the light bound to Him who is the life and the light. This is symbolized on many baptismal fonts that adopt an octagonal figure. The Christian coming to the font will be re-created and now lives in a new day where the endless cycle of broken time is itself broken. Schmemann offers a thought on this view of time:

> Christ rose from the dead on the *first day* after the Sabbath. The life that shone forth from the grave was beyond the inescapable limitations of "seven," of time that leads to death. It was thus the beginning of a new life and of a new time. It was truly the eighth and the first day and it became the day of the Church. The risen Christ, according to the fourth Gospel, appeared to his disciples on the first day and then "after eight days." This is the day on which the Church celebrates the Eucharist—the sacrament of its ascension to the Kingdom and of its participation at the messianic banquet in the "age to come," the day on which the Church fulfills itself as new life.[15]

15. Schmemann's use of "ascension" refers to the repeated theme that runs throughout Scripture which describes God as dwelling "on high." Moses goes up Mount Sinai to meet God. The Israelites go up God's holy mountain to see God in His temple. Thus,

Baptism: The Sacrament of Eternity

The Sunday service becomes a liminal point. It is still the first day of the week and, at the same time, it is a day that goes beyond that week into something truly new.

The eighth day enables Baptism to be a sacrament that sanctifies history. Taking the broken cycle of time and bringing in a new, eternal day is how God takes everything that broke down in the sin of Adam, which followed the seven days of creation, and makes it into something new. Baptism brings that creation and everything in it, us included, to death so that it can be made new and alive again. Luther comments:

> You ask, "How does baptism help me, if it does not altogether blot out and remove sin?" . . . you pledge yourself to continue in this desire, and to slay your sin more and more as long as you live, even until your dying day. This too God accepts. He trains and tests you all your life long, with many good works and with all kinds of sufferings. Thereby he accomplishes what you in baptism have desired, namely, that you may become free from sin, die, and rise again at the Last Day, and so fulfill your baptism. Therefore we read and see how bitterly he has let his saints be tortured, and how much he has let them suffer, in order that, almost slain, they might fulfill the sacrament of baptism, die, and be made new.[16]

Baptism allows death to bring new life and so the end of all we know, found in our death, is brought to us here and now. Instead of endlessly circling through the weeks where each day looks forward to a new day full of sin in this broken world, Baptism sets us on a new course, a tangent that leaps off the circle, never to look back. This brings to mind how Paul continues his discourse in Romans 6: "But now that you have been set free from sin and have become slaves of God, the fruit you get leads to sanctification and its end, eternal life" (v. 22).

---

in the Eucharist, we "go up" to meet God as well. This feature is typically reflected in church architecture as the chancel is set a few steps up from the rest of the sanctuary. (Schmemann, *For the Life of the World*, 63–64. Italics in original.)

16. Luther, *Luther's Works, Vol. 35*, 33–34.

5

Baptism: The Sacrament of Holiness

As I MENTIONED PREVIOUSLY, chrismation (anointing with holy oil) became a rite that developed in the early church. While it was always a distinct act, it was one that was intrinsically linked to Baptism. It is still considered a sacrament in the Orthodox and Catholic churches, but it fails to meet the Lutheran criteria for a sacrament since it has neither a direct command from God to continue doing it and it has no promise of grace and forgiveness attached to it.

It is unfortunate chrismation has broken off into a distinct event. While there is nothing wrong with chrismation, per se, its theological roots are actually baptismal. The Old Testament use of anointing oil directs us to Baptism's role in restoring the image of God. As such, chrismation should never be raised to the level of spiritual equality with Baptism. Its theological foundation is in Baptism and its use should be considered an aspect of Baptism in the same way any of these other themes can be. The divergence of chrismation and Baptism as two separate, if connected, rites splits off a theme that rightly belongs to Baptism and should be considered an aberration.

While chrismation should not be considered a separate event, the theology that has been built up around it can often be folded back into Baptism, where it belongs.[1] That means some of the biblical background

---

1. The use of chrism in different church bodies varies both in theological understanding and liturgical application. This anointing is often done in connection with the baptismal rite, but not always. Schmemann briefly explains the sense of chrismation in the Orthodox Church by saying, "Chrismation is not only an organic part of the

typically thought of as referring to chrismation will instead help us to better understand Baptism.

The primary reference we have for anointing oil is Exodus 30, in the list of items the Israelites were to assemble for use in the tabernacle. While the exact composition is not so useful to us, its purpose is very much applicable to our understanding of Baptism. Anointing differs somewhat from our other themes in Baptism, because its purpose is not to make clean. The recipe God gives for the making of this oil is meant to be unique. It is set apart strictly for God's purposes. God further reinforces this concept by saying it is holy and that it shall be kept as holy. This makes it functionally different from all other oils one might use for any other purpose. This particular oil can only be used at God's direction and for the purposes He outlines.

This oil is given a special function by God. It is used to mark holy things. Before the use of oil, the object could be used for any sort of mundane purpose. Once marked with the oil, the object is openly declared to be God's. He alone owns it and determines what its purpose and function will be. Much of the furniture and utensils used in the tabernacle were anointed with this oil. The altar of incense is marked as holy. It is God's altar, and He determines how and when it shall be used. Any use of it outside of God's prescribed purposes threatens to desecrate the altar and constitutes man's attempt to steal something from God. Leviticus 10 tells the account of Aaron's sons offering incense in contravention of God's outlined usage, which leads to swift and decisive consequences.

An even more relevant connection can be followed when we look at how God uses His holy oil with people. Backing up to Exodus 29 gives us the details of the consecration of priests of the Israelites. All the trappings of the priestly office are put on those who will be consecrated. All their garments are holy and only to be used in the priestly context and only for the purposes God outlines. Of particular interest here are verses 7–9 and 21: "You shall take the anointing oil and pour it on his head and anoint him. Then you shall bring his sons and put coats on them, and you shall gird Aaron and his sons with sashes and bind caps on them. And the priesthood shall be theirs by a statute forever. Thus you shall ordain Aaron and his son . . . Then you shall take part of the blood that is on the altar, and of the anointing oil, and sprinkle it on Aaron and his garments, and on his sons

---

baptismal mystery: it is performed as the fulfillment of Baptism" (Schmemann, *Of Water and The Spirit*, 77).

and his sons' garments with him. He and his garments shall be holy, and his sons and his sons' garments with him."

The anointing oil is poured on Aaron and his sons, and they are ordained into the priesthood. The oil is poured on the priestly garments, and they are marked as holy. This rite is how the priesthood is known in Israel. This rite was meant to be used for every priest who served in the tabernacle and the temple until the day when Christ came and the Old Testament priesthood was brought to a close. We have already looked at how Baptism brings us back into that role of priest through our restoration to the image of God.

The church rightly refers to this sacrament as Holy Baptism. It does so because the church acknowledges and trusts in God's promise to work through the water. The water that had, moments before, been common water, suitable for sustaining earthly life, is now filled with the creative power of the Spirit and is made suitable for sustaining eternal life. The water is set apart by God and for His use. Luther remarks:

> I therefore admonish you again that these two, the Word and the water, must by no means be separated from each other. For where the Word is separated from the water, the water is no different from the water that the maid uses for cooking and could indeed be called a bath-keeper's baptism. But when the Word is with it according to God's ordinance, baptism is a sacrament, and it is called Christ's baptism. This is the first point to be emphasized: the nature and dignity of the holy sacrament (LC IV).[2]

The water is claimed by God, who then uses that water to claim a person as His own. Luther also says, "For he who is a Christian enters with the Lord Christ into a sharing of all His goods. Now since Christ is holy, he, too, must be holy, or he must deny that Christ is holy. If you have been baptized, you have put on the holy garment, which is Christ, as Paul says (Gal. 3:27). The little word 'holy' designates that which is God's own and is due to Him alone."[3] His promise and declaration empower the activity. The fact that the water was mundane prior to this is irrelevant. Now it is God's and by the work of the Spirit it is capable of great things.

Thus it should be no surprise that water, set apart by God for special use, should likewise mark its recipient as holy as well. In Aaron's case, the holy oil meant being marked for the holy priesthood of God. In truth, the

---

2 Kolb et al., *The Book of Concord*, 459.
3. Luther, *Luther's Works, Vol. 30*, 32.

entire nation of Israel was marked as a "holy nation," as it was intended to act as priests before the rest of the world, carrying out the priestly vocation on behalf of the nations around it. Aaron and his sons would be priests in the midst of a nation of priests. The rest of Israel would continue living and working in their earthly vocations while functioning as priests when the opportunity arose. Aaron would fill this role full time, continuously standing as priest before Israel and before the world. Luther explains:

> A new creation, by which the image of God is renewed (Col. 3:10), does not happen by the sham or pretense of some sort of outward works, because in Christ Jesus neither circumcision nor uncircumcision counts; but it is "created after the likeness of God in righteousness and holiness" (Eph. 4:24). When works are performed, they do indeed give a new outward appearance, which captures the attention of the world and the flesh. But they do not produce a new creation, for the heart remains as wicked and as filled with contempt of God and unbelief as it was before. Thus a new creation is a work of the Holy Spirit, who implants a new intellect and will and confers the power to curb the flesh and to flee the righteousness and wisdom of the world.[4]

The holiness given through the gift of the Spirit and the restoration of the image of God, a new creation given to us, all of which are woven together and given through the covenantal act of Baptism, the antitype of Old Testament circumcision. Nowhere else are all of these threads connected and so we cannot help but see them as not two separate themes, but all part of the baptismal whole.

Viewed in terms of this ordination and establishment as priest, the roles of water and oil become identical. Whether one looks to the anointing of Exodus 29 or to the re-creative themes of water we have already examined, particularly in reference to the image of God, both accomplish the same goal. God is both establishing a Christian as a priest in His service and giving him or her the ability to fill the role in which He has placed them. Thus, what we find here in Aaron's ordination is the same kind of resetting action God uses in the other Old Testament baptismal events. Here we simply find a specific subset of people explicitly declared to be priests. However, as stated previously, the entire nation of Israel was a nation of priests and set apart as holy. All of Israel had been baptized in the Red Sea. That means Aaron's ordination is nothing more than a visible demonstration of

---

4. Luther, *Luther's Works*, Vol. 27, 139–140.

what had already happened to all the people present there. As such, this anointing becomes another tributary of the river of baptismal themes we have been exploring.

The reason why oil can be used here as a theme for Baptism instead of water is because we are examining a subtly different idea.[5] When water is involved, we naturally think of the purposes we use it for in everyday life, in particular drinking and washing. Water sustains life and water makes things clean. In the case of anointing, neither of those uses concerns us. The oil used in anointing accomplishes through marking what water accomplishes through re-creation, namely the reestablishment of mankind as priests before God.

The benefit of oil in this instance is its persistence. Oil provides a visual and tactile indication both to the person who has been anointed and to all those around him. For as long as the oil remains, it is a visible reminder that this person has been anointed and set apart for a special purpose. This builds on the ongoing aspect of Baptism. Though the event itself may be over, the mark remains.

This mark carries a dual meaning, with different theologians variously preferring one or the other. First, being baptized into Christ's death means being a recipient of the cross and all it entails. We die to sin and, in that death, we are set apart from the world. We bear the mark of that cross, showing that we have died already and are looking beyond that death to new life. The world reviles us because it cannot destroy us. It assaults us in any manner it can, but it does so fruitlessly. Paul describes bearing the marks of Jesus on his body in Galatians 6, to which Luther responds, "These are the true stigmata, that is, imprinted marks, about which the apostle is speaking here; we, too, by the grace of God, bear them on our body today on account of Christ. For the world persecutes and slays us; false brethren hate us bitterly; and Satan terrifies us inwardly in our hearts with his

---

5. It is worth noting as well that Jesus is known to be the Savior primarily through His title as the Messiah, the Christ, the Anointed One. We find this coming to pass at His Baptism, where He is anointed with the Holy Spirit through His washing with water. Yet, nowhere in the life of Christ do we find Him being anointed with oil in connection with the Holy Spirit. The Spirit makes His grand entrance into the life of Christ here at His Baptism and only here. To state that the oil of chrismation is meant to be the vehicle of the Holy Spirit, as the Catholic and Orthodox claim, simply does not follow from the example of the Anointed One's own life.

flaming darts (Eph. 6:16)—all this for no other reason than that we teach that Christ is our righteousness and life."[6]

Christ's life was filled with conflict between God and the world and He bore out that conflict in His own flesh in the form of insults, beatings, and bloody death. Our lives carry that very same sign. We have rejected Satan and the world to stand with Christ and thus made them our enemies. Just as the apostles rejoiced in their sufferings because it was on account of Christ, so too do we bear the same marks of Christ as a result of being made holy and set apart from the world around us.

Our Baptism is a decisive declaration by God that we are His. Through that Baptism, we engage in battle with our enemy. Schmemann relates the significance of this idea:

> God alone can preserve us in the predicaments and despair of our earthly pilgrimage and fight. This laying on of hands is thus the "commissioning" of new officers, the receiving by them of their "marching orders," the sign and the gift of that heroism without which there can be no Christian life.[7]

Being set apart by God means we are necessarily soldiers who march for Christ. We have changed our allegiance and we bear the mark of the cross, displaying that allegiance. Every point of our lives will be marked by that conflict as we continue to repel the temptations of the world. The mark of Baptism, as suggested through the act of anointing, becomes a battle scar. It is a sign that you have been joined to Christ's life and death. Everything the world says about Christ and does to Him has and will find its way to you as well. Jesus tells His own disciples the uncomfortable truth in Matthew 10: "A disciple is not above his teacher, nor a servant above his master. It is enough for the disciple to be like his teacher, and the servant like his master. If they have called the master of the house Beelzebul, how much more will they malign those of his household" (vv. 24–25). We will examine Baptism's relationship to discipleship a bit later. For now, it is worth remembering that Baptism joins us to Christ's life in all the ways we might look forward to but also in ways we might rather avoid. Baptism is a package deal, for the act of Baptism is akin to taking the oath upon entering military service. Being baptized means joining the fight in earnest.

---

6. Luther, *Luther's Works*, Vol. 27, 143–4.
7. Schmemann, *Of Water and the Spirit*, 126.

The second meaning associated with this persistent mark we are given is that of ownership. Where the first aspect describes to the world what we are *doing,* the second describes whose we *are*. In that sense, both views of the mark are useful and work together. The first shows us as soldiers marching to war. The second becomes the national flag emblazoned on our uniform that tells the world what side we are on.

In the biblical sense of slavery or servitude, it was not uncommon for servants to be tattooed by their masters to show ownership. It was also normal for Roman soldiers to bear a tattoo marking them as such.[8] This indelible mark expresses quite explicitly the same persistent nature of the anointing. Aaron and his sons were not just anointed as priests but specifically as priests of the God of Israel.

God claims His people and marks them as His own. God tells the Israelites, "For you are a people holy to the Lord your God. The Lord your God has chosen you to be a people for His treasured possession, out of all the peoples who are on the face of the earth" (Deut. 7:6). The nation is holy because it is His. God made sure both the Egyptians and the Israelites knew it and also the other surrounding nations. In Joshua 2, Rahab tells the spies how the fear of the Israelites (and of their God) has fallen upon the nations. God made a public declaration of ownership, both of the nation as a whole and now of His priesthood.

Marking the recipient with the sign of the cross in preparation for Baptism[9] draws on these two ideas we find flowing out of the symbolism of anointing. Of this, Schmemann says, "It is the rite of the Church as she *takes possession* of the child in the name of Christ and engraves him with the Sign of the Cross, the sign of Christ's victory and lordship, and begins to prepare him for baptism."[10] This claim of ownership and being slaves to God recalls Paul's continued discussion in Romans 6, "But now that you have been set free from sin and have become slaves of God, the fruit you get leads to sanctification and its end, eternal life. For the wages of sin is death, but the free gift of God is eternal life in Christ Jesus our Lord" (vv. 22–23). That we will be slaves to something is a given. The question Paul poses is "Whom will you be slaves to?" Our Baptism presents a possibility that was barred to us before: to be slaves to a Master who actually loves us and wants what is best for us.

---

8. Daniélou, *The Bible and the Liturgy*, 55–56.
9. Kolb et al., *The Book of Concord*, 373.
10. Schmemann, *Of Water and the Spirit*, 139. Italics in original.

In this sense, the anointing further signifies the protection of the owner. As in a feudal system where one owes fealty to a lord and is bound to support him and carry out his commands, but where also the lord is bound to defend his vassals, so too does God claim us and pledge to defend us. Luther applies this idea to his daily prayers in the Small Catechism:

> In the evening, when you go to bed, you are to make the sign of the holy cross and say:
>
> "God the Father, Son, and Holy Spirit watch over me. Amen."
>
> Then, kneeling or standing, say the Apostles' Creed and the Lord's Prayer. If you wish, you may in addition recite this little prayer as well:
>
> "I give thanks to you, my heavenly Father, through Jesus Christ your dear Son, that you have graciously protected me today, and I ask you to forgive me all my sins, where I have done wrong, and graciously to protect me tonight. For into your hands I commend myself: my body, my soul, and all that is mine. Let your holy angel be with me, so that the wicked foe may have no power over me. Amen."[11]

Being owned by God is not a restriction but is actually the greatest defense one may have against the assaults of Satan and the temptations of the world. Your baptismal anointing in the priesthood of God is proof of your place in His service. Luther's implication here is that making the sign of the cross is a reminder of whose you are and that He has indeed kept His promise to care for you this day.

Though anointing into the priesthood is the most detailed passage regarding anointing, it is by no means the only anointing that occurs. The kings of Israel (and of other nations) were also anointed by representatives of God, as were prophets. First Kings 1 details the anointing of Solomon as king after his father, David. First Kings 19 has Elijah anointing a new king of Syria, as well as a new king of Israel. Further, Elijah is directed to anoint Elisha as his successor to the office of prophet.

God anoints His prophets, priests, and kings. The allusion to the restoration of the image of God is unmistakable. By being baptized into the life of Christ, we become little Christs, little "anointed ones."[12] That God

---

11. Kolb et al., *The Book of Concord*, 364.
12. As mentioned previously, both the Catholic and Orthodox churches hold

is accomplishing the same work through anointing He does through the other themes of Baptism is likewise unmistakable. For we find passages such as 1 Samuel 16, which tells us, "Then Samuel took the horn of oil and anointed him in the midst of his brothers. And the Spirit of the Lord rushed upon David from that day forward" (v. 13). The Spirit is active and at work through anointing, just as He has been through the other aspects of Baptism. We can tell here that the anointing of prophets, priests, and kings all work similarly and to similar ends. These are people chosen by God for His express purposes, setting them apart for the work He has prepared for them. He claims them as His own and the Spirit guides them and protects them in their work.

All these examples demonstrate that Baptism's purpose is to cleanse us and return us to a state when we were free from sin. In God's judgment against sin, that sin is destroyed and wiped away. Trusting in God's promise means that the righteousness that He has given us remains. His perfect righteousness has no need of judgment and so judgment passes it by. It calls to mind passages such as Malachi 3, "But who can endure the day of His coming, and who can stand when He appears? For He is like a refiner's fire and like fullers' soap. He will sit as a refiner and purifier of silver, and He will purify the sons of Levi and refine them like gold and silver, and they will bring offerings in righteousness to the Lord. Then the offering of Judah and Jerusalem will be pleasing to the Lord as in the days of old and as in former years" (vv. 2–4).

Baptism is meant to cleanse and make pure. The waters of the Flood scour the earth and purge it from the taint of unbelief. To the extent that it is able to, prior to the final destruction of sin, it cleanses the world. It washes away the imperfections and leaves only what is good.

When passages such as Malachi 3 describe this purification in terms of fire, it feels like it should be a separate and unconnected theme, and yet it is not. John the Baptist brings together these seemingly distinct elements when he tells the crowds, "I baptize you with water for repentance, but He who is coming after me is mightier than I, whose sandals I am not worthy to carry. He will baptize you with the Holy Spirit and fire. His winnowing fork

---

chrismation/Confirmation as a separate sacrament. Given that anointing uses a different medium than Baptism typically does, oil versus water, it is easy to see why the two might be seen as distinct. However, all of the theology usually associated with anointing is already found in Baptism. Furthermore, the biblical witness and the witness of the early church always associated Jesus' Baptism with the point at which He properly becomes the Christ, the Anointed One, an action carried out not with oil but with water.

is in His hand, and He will clear His threshing floor and gather His wheat into the barn, but the chaff He will burn with unquenchable fire" (Matt. 3:11–12). Gathering the wheat and burning the chaff may be a different image than we would expect for Baptism, but the result of the Flood is the same. The "wheat" was gathered in the ark while the "chaff" was drowned in the water. John's words carry a tone of finality, pointing forward to the culmination of everything Baptism seeks to accomplish in creation and in the lives of God's people. Jesus will baptize with fire and the world will be fully and completely clean.

One might question why God uses fire as a theme for Baptism, when water is used nearly everywhere else. However, we have already seen how oil is also used to convey baptismal themes. Water carries the deep and abiding connection to life in creation. Water is necessary for life and sustains all life. A Baptism with water is a rite in which we can safely participate. Fire is the domain of God. God descends on Mount Sinai in fire in Exodus 19. God sends fire down from heaven to accept Elijah's offering in 1 Kings 18. The fire on God's holy altar consumes the offerings brought by His people. Fire brings God's judgment so creation may be made pure.

Though God's use of water makes the connection to Baptism clearer, it is really the purpose of what takes place that unites the activity with that of Baptism. God does not restrict Himself to water as He teaches us about Baptism, so this should not take us entirely by surprise. Whether in water or in fire, God's divine power is made manifest and His purpose is the same.

Fire, water, and oil are all used to restore people and that restoration is accomplished by removing that which is sinful. In Genesis 1 and 2, all creation was holy for all of it was God's. Sin is separation from God, so making something holy is nothing more than bringing it back to where it belongs. God sees that a gracious accommodation is necessary for this sinful world. He separates those things that are used for common and mundane purposes from those that are used to convey His grace. In the new creation there will be no need for common items because God's grace will be everywhere and filling everything, just as it did in the Garden of Eden.

If fire is a sign and indication of God's presence, then the use of fire in the life of a person indicates the presence and work of God within that person. God claims the sacrifices offered at the temple in fire from the holy altar. Fire is the sign of God's acceptance of the sacrifice and of the person offering it.

When the sacrifice that is offered is a person, such as is the case in Holy Baptism, the theme of fire is just as valid. Whether one thinks in terms of water washing away the taint of sin or in terms of fire refining out the imperfections, they both accomplish the desired goal. Both express the need to remove sin. God expresses many ways in which people are prepared to return to His presence and restored to the relationships and vocations they were created to hold.

This concept of holiness then allows us to fully understand the ramifications of Peter's message as he references God's declaration to the Israelites in Exodus 19, "But you are a chosen race, a royal priesthood, a holy nation, a people for his own possession, that you may proclaim the excellencies of him who called you out of darkness into his marvelous light" (1 Pet. 2:9). The Levitical laws of the Old Testament were meant not to be punitive but instructive. They were meant to help the people live as though they were holy, as set apart from all the other people on earth. Repeatedly throughout the books of Leviticus and Deuteronomy we find God saying such things as "Speak to all the congregation of the people of Israel and say to them, You shall be holy, for I the Lord your God am holy" (Lev. 19:2) or "For you are a people holy to the Lord your God, and the Lord has chosen you to be a people for His treasured possession, out of all the peoples who are on the face of the earth" (Deut. 14:2).

This set-apart status was essential to who they were. Peter indicates this holy quality is still present in the church today. We as the church are separate and distinct from every other organization and people group in the world. We have been claimed by God as His treasured possession. He alone guides and dictates who we are and what we do. The more we look and act like those around us, the less we resemble who we have been made to be as God's people.

Luther puts Exodus 19 and 1 Peter together as he expounds on Titus 2:

> In Exodus (Ex. 19:5): "You shall be peculiar to Me, a peculiar people." We say "My own," and Peter says (1 Peter 2:9) "a people for His possession." Vergil speaks of the *peculium*. That is, this is a people which is the property of Christ, in whose midst He dwells, which is devoted to Him, which He looks after as He would a flock, to which He has given life. Not only has He rescued it, but He purifies it every day if there is any filth left. Likewise, *who are zealous [for good deeds]*, who with rivalry, zeal, and competition strive to do good works. Here he returns to the first point. We have

been redeemed, and we are purified daily in order that we may live in good works.[13]

The Israelites' holy status was given to them by virtue of God's work in the Passover and all of the following events leading up to their arrival at Mount Sinai. Here He gives them His Law. Through the command God gave to Abraham to circumcise his male descendants, He had already given them one means by which the world would see them as different and distinct. Through the Law at Mount Sinai and now in Christ, God's people learn what it means to live as holy and are given the ability to carry out the calling we have been given.

Luther notes the dual vocation of priest and king spelled out by Peter:

> Not only are we the freest of kings, we are also priests forever, which is far more excellent than being kings, for as priests we are worthy to appear before God to pray for others and to teach one another divine things. These are the functions of priests, and they cannot be granted to any unbeliever. Thus Christ has made it possible for us, provided we believe in him, to be not only his brethren, co-heirs, and fellow-kings, but also his fellow-priests. Therefore we may boldly come into the presence of God in the spirit of faith and cry "Abba, Father!" pray for one another, and do all things which we see done and foreshadowed in the outer and visible works of priests.[14]

Through Christ we are given the authority and responsibility to extend His spiritual kingdom and to live out the rulership we were given in the beginning. We also see our position as priests restored. We are both and called to live as both. This royal priesthood is something only possible for one who has been set apart by God for this special purpose. The anointing we are given in Baptism signifies God's claim over us, just as the anointings in the Old Testament designated the various prophets, priests, and kings as chosen by Him for their respective roles. Schmemann comments further:

> "Royal Priesthood"—not kingship alone and not priesthood alone, but their belonging together as the fulfillment of one in the other, the realization of the one by the other—such is the mystery of man revealed in Christ. If the property of the king is to have power and dominion, that of the priest is to offer sacrifice, i.e. to be mediator between God and creation, the "sanctifier" of life through its

13. Luther, *Luther's Works, Vol. 29*, 67.
14. Luther, *Luther's Works, Vol. 31*, 355.

> inclusion into the divine will and order. This double function is man's from the very beginning, but precisely as one function, in which man's natural kingship is fulfilled in priesthood, in which his natural priesthood makes him the king of creation. He has "power and dominion" over the world, but he fulfills this power by *sanctifying* the world, by making it into communion with God. Not only is his power from God and under God, but it has God as its goal and content, as that ultimate *good* which, as we have seen, constitutes the inner law of all power.[15]

As priests and kings, and prophets as well, we are sent into the world to bring the world back to God. Each of the three anointed vocations carries this out in a slightly different way, but each is dependent upon the others and works jointly with them. Thus, each of these vocations is merely a part of what it means to be holy and is a function of living in the image of God.

Just as we reflect God back to Himself as we are clothed in Christ, so too do we stand as a reflection of God before the world. We must be holy, as God is holy, if we are to carry out this work. We can only have dominion over creation as kings if we do so according to the order and command of the Creator and King of kings. We can only proclaim God's prophetic, promise-filled Word if we keep that proclamation distinct from the false and fallible promises made everywhere else in the world. We can only call down blessings upon the world if we direct our prayers to the one God capable of hearing them and responding to them.

And so our vocation as anointed workers in God's kingdom, as people restored to His image, necessitates holiness. We are set apart, not just to look different but to display in word and deed what makes us different from the rest of the people in the world, just as God Himself is different from all other gods. Holiness and the image of God go hand in hand, and both draw us back to the point at which they are restored to us in Baptism.

---

15. Schmemann, *Of Water and the Spirit*, 95–96. Italics in original.

6

Baptism: The Sacrament of Passage

THE EARLY CHURCH FATHERS were split in their interpretation of the Passover event. A great number of them saw the Passover as baptismal in nature.[1] Of special importance in this event was the function of the lamb's blood. Judgment, in the form of the destroying angel, came down on the land. Those who rested under the protection of the blood found they were safe while the rest of the land suffered under the devastation.

While the blood of the lamb might make you think in terms of the Eucharist, and not without merit, the activity taking place has a distinctly baptismal feel to it. God binds Himself to a promise that those under the blood are safe from destruction. The language is very reminiscent of that used of the covenantal sign of the rainbow following the Flood. The rainbow and the blood are signs for death to pass by, that those who are under it are safe from whatever else may be happening in the world.

Again, the trust must be there for the blood to do its work. Like Noah, who trusted God's instructions instead of choosing not to build the ark, the Israelites must have trusted God to save them through the blood of the lamb. Had they chosen not to go through with it, the judgment that

---

1. The Eucharist themes of Passover abound as well, leading other theologians to direct their thoughts that way. With the unleavened bread, the lamb, and the blood taking center stage in the salvific work of Passover, it is easy to see why one might think this way. That is especially true given the context of the Last Supper. In reality, much of what transpires in the Passover relates very closely to other baptismal themes. Given the weightiness of the event, it is not surprising that themes for both sacraments might be woven throughout and seeing the event in light of either or both sacraments can be convincingly argued.

came upon the land would have struck them with just as much force as it had the Egyptians. These protective coverings, found both here and in the rainbow, all relate to the same baptismal idea of putting on Christ. By putting on Christ, judgment that falls against sin naturally passes by because, in Christ, we are seen as sinless and judgment is unnecessary.

Freed from judgment by the Passover, the Israelites move on to where they will be free from slavery as well. The crossing of the Red Sea, inextricably bound as it is to the Passover, makes the entire event one of the most momentous in the Old Testament. The ten dreadful plagues and the final release of the Israelites culminates here. As the Israelites think they are finally free, they find Pharaoh is not quite done with them and God is not quite done with Pharaoh. The Israelites cry to God for salvation and God hears them. God intervenes so as to demonstrate His power to save and His power over all creation, even over life and death.

Luther asserts the connection between the crossing and Baptism as well when he says in his Flood Prayer, "... and who drowned Pharaoh with his army in the Red Sea and led your people Israel through the same sea on dry ground, thereby prefiguring this bath of your Holy Baptism ..."[2] There are certainly some similar ideas to what we see happening in other Baptism-related events. God uses a colossal amount of water to keep His people safe from unrighteous people.[3]

Strangely, the comparisons between the crossing and the Flood do not go much beyond a broad concept of salvation and the use of water. Noah was not in any personal danger that we are told about. God wanted to keep him safe from the judgment that would be falling on everyone else. The list of the world's crimes in Genesis 6 include man's great wickedness, evil thoughts, and violence. Certainly, a lack of faith is the root of the world's problems here, but the evil is diffuse and generalized. Noah may have harbored some uncertainty when the storms raged, but at that point he was already safe.

The crossing of the Red Sea has a very different feel to it. For the Israelites, their salvation from slavery was a very personal thing, and the work of God through Moses affected them in a rather immediate sense. Freedom from slavery simply is not a theme we find in the Flood account, yet it is

---

2. Kolb et al., *The Book of Concord*, 373–74.

3. We find here as well that faith precedes Baptism. The Israelites trusted in God to save, as evidenced in the Passover. They did not come to the shores of the Red Sea to finally put their trust in Him. The process of their salvation was already underway by the time they arrive at the Red Sea.

central to the crossing. The crossing is the culmination of all the work God had done for them since the beginning of Exodus. The Israelites have been trusting in God thus far, as evidenced by their actions during the Passover. Now God completes this work through Moses, proving Himself truly a God worthy of worship, unlike the false gods of Egypt, and destroying His enemies while simultaneously saving His own people.

Those being judged here are not dealing in some generalized violence and evil. The threat of Pharaoh is very specific. He means to keep them enslaved forever, every man, woman, and child withering under his bootheel until they die. Were God to fail at His task here, the Israelites would have nothing to look forward to but a dark future in a pagan land until they faded away entirely.

However, as at the time of the Flood, God's promise and man's faith in that promise both take center stage once more. Luther comments on Moses, "Then Moses cried to the Lord. His heart must have pounded and trembled a little, so that God chided him in His anger, saying: 'Why do you cry to Me?' (Ex. 14:15). Yes, he was looking for a way to rescue the nation from the hands of the enemy; for they were surrounded by death."[4] Like a pastor holding the head of a new Christian over the waters of the font, Moses allows God to work through him. "Thus we, too, must cleave to the Word of God through faith. By means of a little word of God, 'Strike the sea with your rod!' Moses blazed a dry trail through the sea in a moment. One could never have drained the sea with a hundred thousand ships, but God accomplished this feat with a single word!"[5]

Forgiveness could be considered one of the ongoing benefits of this Baptism in the Red Sea, as it establishes a special relationship between God and His people. God uses this event as the foundation for that relationship and reiterates it numerous times. "I am the Lord your God, who brought you out of the land of Egypt, out of the house of slavery" (Ex. 20:2) is how God confirms His authority as He gives the Israelites the Ten Commandments. This does mean the relationship, which began with the exodus, has a baptismal component and that component brings with it God's grace and forgiveness. Many times Israel sins and arouses God to anger, but He refrains from simply blotting them out because they are His people. It is only when they finally reject Him entirely that He does exact His judgment against them, and even then not for quite a while.

4. Luther, *Luther's Works, Vol. 22*, 310
5. Luther, *Luther's Works, Vol. 22*, 310–11

However, the theme prevailing in the crossing itself is not forgiveness but freedom and life. God uses the event to bring His people out of slavery to freedom, out of death to life. We have heard what Paul says in Romans 6:4: "We were buried therefore with Him by baptism into death, in order that, just as Christ was raised from the dead by the glory of the Father, we too might walk in newness of life." But let us not forget the explanation continues:

> For if we have been united with Him in a death like His, we shall certainly be united with Him in a resurrection like His. We know that our old self was crucified with Him in order that the body of sin might be brought to nothing, so that we would no longer be enslaved to sin. For one who has died has been set free from sin. Now if we have died with Christ, we believe that we will also live with Him. We know that Christ, being raised from the dead, will never die again; death no longer has dominion over Him. (Rom. 6:5–9)

The old life of the Israelites died in the Red Sea, along with Pharaoh and his armies. The one who would bring death to God's people instead found himself drowned and dead. They have been set free, no longer subject to slavery. They will no longer be residents in a pagan and unrighteous land among a pagan and unrighteous people. In fact, they are forbidden from even considering it an option, for to do so would be to reject the Baptism they were given in the Red Sea.

The crossing demonstrates the aspect of Baptism as passage. Schmemann comments on the place of Easter Vigil within the baptismal rites of the early church:

> And this "catechetical," pre-baptismal element is still evident in the Vespers of the Great and Holy Saturday, more especially in the fifteen lessons from the Old Testament, all of which are "paradigms" not only of the Resurrection but also of Baptism, or rather of *salvation* as *passage*—from slavery to freedom, from death to life, from earth into heaven.[6]

Rarely in the modern church is Baptism thought of as a transition into something truly new. Who you were is now left behind. Everything that marked your old life is wiped away. You have gone from slavery to freedom. You are free from slavery to sin and death. God now guides you in the way that leads to eternal life.

---

6. Schmemann, *Of Water and the Spirit*, 113. Italics in original.

Baptism: The Sacrament of Passage

Though the crossing of the Red Sea would imply an end to the exodus and a transition to the next phase of Israelite life, that is not exactly true. The Passover that immediately preceded the crossing came with a promise of its own. Moses says to the people, "And when the Lord brings you into the land of the Canaanites, the Hittites, the Amorites, the Hivites, and the Jebusites, which He swore to your fathers to give you, a land flowing with milk and honey, you shall keep this service in this month" (Ex. 13:5). Before they have even left Egypt, the Israelites are already given a promise. In fact, the restorative and re-creative work of God is visible here again.

Prior to the children of Abraham taking up residence in Egypt, they lived peacefully in the land of Canaan. Now God is resetting them, winding time back to when they dwelled in that land so that they may dwell in the land once more. The eighth day returns in this promise as well, not explicitly, but by virtue of what we have seen the eighth day doing elsewhere. While the Israelites will return to their land, they do so as different people. Soon they will have the tabernacle and the ark of the covenant. Soon they will have the priesthood and will celebrate the festivals that remember God's gracious work. In short, while the Israelites will return to an approximation of the life they had prior to their stay in Egypt, things will be better this time around. God will be with them in a new and special way. They will get to interact with God in a way Abraham never did.

Everything that began with the crossing of the Red Sea finally culminates in the, less momentous but no less miraculous, crossing of the Jordan River in Joshua 3. As the priests carrying the ark enter the Jordan, all the waters pile up and allow the people to cross on dry ground. The similarity to the Red Sea is obvious.

Baptismal theology connects here in a slightly different way. Here, the Israelites are not fleeing from anything and the narrative does not indicate they are in need of saving. Rather, the idea of passage comes through once more. Israel finally transitions from their wandering lifestyle to truly becoming recipients of God's promise and living in the land in which God chooses to dwell. This transitional aspect of Baptism is commented on by Schmemann:

> In it the new life received in Baptism and sealed in the holy anointment is revealed in its dynamic; not static, essence—revealed as an end always transformed into beginning, as indeed a passage,

the "passage" from "this world" into the Kingdom of God, as a "procession" toward the day without evening of God's eternity.[7]

Though the people who have come through the waters of Baptism are re-created, that does not mean the work done within them and around them is complete. Their lives are reset in order that they may then proceed forward toward the fulfillment of the promise for which they have been prepared. In this case, the Israelites' Baptism in the Red Sea and subsequent Baptism in the Jordan was a preparation for their eventual residence in the temporal kingdom of God, the land where God Himself dwelled in a special way.

Schmemann draws the idea of transition and procession out further when he says:

> It connects Baptism, the sacrament of regeneration, with the Eucharist, the sacrament of the Church: the sacrament which fulfills the Church as the presence and the gift in "this world" of the Kingdom of God.[8]

With the Red Sea and the Jordan as bookends for the Israelites' journey, the entire forty years in the wilderness becomes one long Baptism. The Israelites are saved from Pharaoh and slavery, but they have not yet begun to be the new people God intends for them to be. The forty years becomes the long resetting and re-creating process. This is further driven home as Joshua and Caleb end up being the only two to set foot in the Promised Land. The forty years in the wilderness also brings to mind the forty days of the Flood, a parallel that now seems not so coincidental. God purges the sinful apostasy and unbelief from His people and those who are finally drawn through the waters are those who trust God and follow Him.

This extended baptismal interlude also explains the placement of Baptism within the life of the Christian and of the church. As shown previously, Baptism necessarily follows faith but also precedes the Eucharist. My experience has found that many Christians cannot articulate why you are baptized before you come to the Lord's Table. There is just a vague sense that it would not be proper.

Though a case can be made for why faith, then Baptism, then finally Communion is the proper order, the two crossings show this reasoning better than any other. The Red Sea sets out with God's promise and the

7. Schmemann, *Of Water and the Spirit*, 115.
8. Schmemann, *Of Water and the Spirit*, 115.

Baptism: The Sacrament of Passage

Jordan brings us to fulfillment, as God's people finally set foot in the land where the temple will be built where God will dwell. God's promise was not a generalized promise of salvation, peace, or prosperity. Instead, God promised His people a land of their own. More importantly, it would be the place God would set up a permanent residence and where His people were *meant* to dwell.

As the place where God rules over His people, the analogy to the kingdom of God Jesus repeatedly refers to is visibly established. It is by living in God's presence that a group of people becomes *God's* people. Moses himself argues the point with God on Mount Sinai. "And [Moses] said to [God], 'If Your presence will not go with me, do not bring us up from here. For how shall it be known that I have found favor in Your sight, I and Your people? Is it not in Your going with us, so that we are distinct, I and Your people, from every other people on the face of the earth?'" (Ex. 33:15–16). For God to be able to dwell with anyone, they must be made into people who are capable of being in His presence without being destroyed. Baptism is the means by which God brings about that transformative restoration and enables someone to be there safely.

It is by coming into God's presence that we become God's people, that we *become* the church of God. Paul adds, "So then you are no longer strangers and aliens, but you are fellow citizens with the saints and members of the household of God, built on the foundation of the apostles and prophets, Christ Jesus Himself being the cornerstone, in whom the whole structure, being joined together, grows into a holy temple in the Lord. In Him you also are being built together into a dwelling place for God by the Spirit" (Eph. 2:19–22). We are built on Christ through the work of the Spirit. Nowhere is Christ more visible than in His own body and blood, which then makes the Eucharist the sacrament which ultimately founds and establishes the church.[9] Schmemann shows the progression:

> In Baptism we are born again of Water and the Spirit, and it is this birth which makes us *open* to the gift of the Holy Spirit, to our personal Pentecost. And finally it is the gift of the Holy Spirit

---

9. Since the Eucharist is the physical presence of God, it is the sacrament that, beyond anything else, completes what God's plan intends in this life. Faith and the cleansing of Baptism are a part of the salvific process because they are directed toward this entry into God's presence. Salvation is not ultimately about forgiveness but *reunification with God*, for which forgiveness is a means to that end.

that "opens" to us access to the Church, to Christ's table in His Kingdom.[10]

We will examine the Spirit's involvement in Baptism a bit later. For now, it suffices to say that Baptism is what prepares the Christian for participation in the Eucharist. Just as the leper needed cleansing before being readmitted to God's presence and just as the Israelites needed their forty-year Baptism before entering the Promised Land, Christians need to be cleansed in the waters of Baptism before they can safely appear before God, as Leviticus 16 outlines. Baptism continues the salvific work begun by God through His gift of faith which trusts in His promise of grace and life. Baptism expands our ability to participate in the life of Christ. It also guides us in how to begin living out that life in the world.

As with the baptismal themes that preceded the Red Sea and the Jordan, the relationships founded in this Baptism all work similarly. God establishes a covenant and promise with His people. Even when they sin with outright and unabashed idolatry, His promise still stands. They are disciplined, but they do repent of their actions and are forgiven. At no point in the journey does God abandon them or leave them to their own devices, despite their constant haranguing. They have been baptized. They are His people. Their eventual rejection by Him is simply a response to the rejection they had already given Him. By rejecting God, their baptismal covenant no longer defends them. They chose to jump over the side of the ark into the floodwaters and hope for the best.

Likewise, our Baptism works as a sign and assurance that we are righteous before God and that we live our life in His presence. As Luther puts it, "Thus, we must regard baptism and put it to use in such a way that we may draw strength and comfort from it when our sins or conscience oppress us, and say: 'But I am baptized! And if I have been baptized, I have the promise that I shall be saved and have eternal life, both in soul and body (LC IV).[11]

There is one further point which illustrates this transitional aspect of Baptism. We look again at what Paul says in Romans 6: "We were buried therefore with Him by baptism into death, in order that, just as Christ was raised from the dead by the glory of the Father, we too might walk in newness of life" (v. 4). The sin we inherited from Adam leads inexorably to death. Paul's words connect Baptism to death. Luther uses this language himself repeatedly, such as in his discussion of Baptism in the Small Catechism:

10. Schmemann, *Of Water and the Spirit*, 116. Italics in original.
11. Kolb et al., *The Book of Concord*, 462.

Baptism: The Sacrament of Passage

> *What does such baptizing with water signify?* Answer: It signifies that the old Adam in us should, by daily contrition and repentance, be drowned and die with all sins and evil lusts. And also it shows that a new man should daily come forth and arise, who shall live before God in righteousness and purity forever.[12]

Baptism means death, specifically our death. It means dying to sin and rising to new life. That means every Christian who comes to the font is coming to a watery coffin, a basin in which they will be buried. Baptism becomes our participation in Christ's death so that we rise from that watery grave living then in Christ's resurrection.

That Baptism equates to death is not new to Luther, though he does expound upon this connection at length. Through our participation in Christ's death, our sin is nailed to the cross, dies, and is buried right alongside the Christ who knew no sin and was made to be sin. Thus, in Christ's resurrection, we too rise, righteous before God. However, Paul's equation in Romans 6 works both ways. If Baptism is equated with death, then *death* can be equated with *Baptism*. If, in Baptism, I die with Christ and rise again, then my death will be no more an obstacle to me than my Baptism. If I had nothing to worry about approaching the font to receive the gracious sacramental gift, then I certainly have nothing to worry about when my death approaches. My body's physical death will be little more than a speed bump in my life, for my eternal life does not start at the moment of physical death. I already died in my Baptism, which means I am already living my eternal life *now*.

This is evidenced in the daily struggle with sin we all face. The death we die is a daily one as Baptism continuously brings about our sanctification. Luther describes this in his Small Catechism:

> For without the Word of God the water is simple water and no Baptism. But with the Word of God it is a Baptism, that is, a gracious water of life and a washing of regeneration in the Holy Spirit. As Paul says in Titus chapter 3, "He saved us . . . by the washing of regeneration and renewal of the Holy Spirit, whom He poured out on us richly through Jesus Christ our Savior, so that being justified by His grace we might become heirs according to the hope of eternal life."[13]

---

12. Kolb et al., *The Book of Concord*, 360.
13. Kolb et al., *The Book of Concord*, 359.

Our Baptism is made a constant part of our life as Christ continues to be a part of everything we do. Every day we rise is a day we rise in Christ; the resurrection becomes present once again. We die to sin each day, but already that death does not mean the end of us. Our lives already continue and our Baptism is still there every morning. If we are spiritually dying to sin now through our Baptism, then we can be confident our physical death will be no greater hindrance to us when the time comes.

7

Baptism: The Sacrament of Re-Creation

JESUS' OWN BAPTISM IS the first narrative event in the New Testament that clearly connects to Baptism. When asked where one might look to find out about Baptism, many Christians think of this event first. Unfortunately, Jesus' Baptism does not tell us a great deal unless we weave together the Old Testament threads that have led us to this point.

John the Baptist, who has been busy preparing the way for Christ, is well acquainted with the theology of the Old Testament. When Jesus comes to John to be baptized, John understands immediately that this is not how things should work. Jesus, by virtue of His perfect and uncorrupted nature, has never been in spiritual slavery in Egypt. He does not number among the unrighteous who are washed away in the Flood. Jesus is not a spiritual leper cut off from the presence of God. Jesus has never been dirty, and thus never needs to be washed clean. Luther expresses a similar thought:

> But when John beheld the heaven opening over the Baptism of Christ, heard the voice of the Father, and saw the Holy Spirit descend in the form of a dove—when he witnessed this magnificent spectacle, then John was convinced that this was the Messiah. And John was seized with a sense of deep humility, awe, and reverence, thinking: "Lo, did I baptize Him over whom the heavens open?" This prompted him to exclaim: "Indeed, I should be baptized by You, whereas You ask me to baptize You." Therefore the Lord replied: "Let it be so now" (Matt. 3:15); then He stepped out of the water and went about His mission.[1]

---

1. Luther, *Luther's Works, Vol. 22*, 160.

Indeed, the entire course of action is backward. Jesus should be baptizing everyone else, yet He is the one who steps into the water to receive the Baptism. But, it must be so, as Jesus Himself explains. It is "to fulfill all righteousness" (Matt. 3:15), not on His behalf but ours. Jesus restarts the creation process and creates a place where the righteousness of creation exists once again.

The substitutionary aspect of Jesus' Baptism is certainly prominent. Paul's words about being joined to the death and resurrection of Christ through Baptism come through here loud and clear. For Baptism to be effective for our salvation, God must first make it capable of doing so. Due to his continuous wrangling with the other Reformers, Luther likes hitting on this particular point repeatedly:

> Therefore it is not simply a natural water, but a divine, heavenly, holy, and blessed water—praise it in any other terms you can—all by virtue of the Word, which is a heavenly, holy Word that no one can sufficiently extol, for it contains and conveys all that is God's. This, too, is where it derives its nature so that it is called a sacrament, as St. Augustine taught, "Accedat verbum ad elementum et fit sacramentum," which means that "when the Word is added to the element or the natural substance, it becomes a sacrament," that is, a holy, divine thing and sign (LC IV).[2]

God's Word of promise is what both activates and validates the water as the vehicle by which every blessing and promise given through the baptismal themes of the Old Testament finally come to us.

The central concept of re-creation finds its focus here. The beginning of Jesus' ministry is found here in the Jordan, in the midst of the waters of Baptism. John reminds us of this: "In the beginning was the Word, and the Word was with God, and the Word was God" (John 1:1). Jesus, the Word, is added to the water and the water is made holy. God enters the water, not in some allegorical sense but in person. Through God's promise of creation and re-creation, life and eternal life, every baptismal theme of the Old Testament is funneled right to this point. All of it is narrowed to a pinpoint focus on this one moment, on the person of Christ. From that point, the action moves outward again to all those who would later be baptized. Recall Paul's words from Romans 6: we are bound through our Baptism not simply to Christ's death but also to His resurrection and *life*. That makes everything Jesus did ours as well. It is because Jesus was the perfect prophet,

---

2. Kolb et al., *The Book of Concord*, 459.

priest, and king that we also become that through our Baptism. It is because Jesus is the perfect child of God that we, too, can be counted as such. It is because of Christ that we are even capable of being perfect. It is here that passages such as Hebrews 5:9–10 become true for us: "And being made perfect, He became the source of eternal salvation to all who obey Him, being designated by God a high priest after the order of Melchizedek." Jesus follows the template of Melchizedek as priest and king both chronologically and as the fulfillment of the kingship and priesthood Melchizedek held. Through our Baptism into Christ, we are given the ability to be both priest and king, too, as we are anointed with the waters of Baptism. Jesus fulfills all righteousness here by bringing us back to the righteousness humanity once had. John the Baptist's confusion is understandable but, seen from the perspective of God's re-creative activity, it was the only way it could happen.

The significance of Jesus' Baptism does not end with making the waters effective for our use. God demonstrates here, once and for all, what the purpose of Baptism is. The Old Testament themes have centered on this idea of re-creation, of bringing God's people back before the Fall when they were righteous. Genesis 1 describes the triune God presiding over the raw stuff of His creation, with the Spirit hovering over the waters, the Father directing the activity and speaking Christ, the Word, into the unformed universe. Here at Jesus' Baptism, Jesus steps into the water, the heavens open and the Father speaks, and the Spirit descends, hovering over Christ in the water. The very beginning of creation in miniature is played out before John and the assembled crowd. Jesus marks where the new creation begins, both in time and space. He creates a bridge between the creation of the world and this moment in history through His Baptism and locates the fountain and foundation of that new creation in Himself.

The appearance of the Trinity is not random or accidental. The triune God shows Himself in all three persons to impress upon us the magnitude of what is taking place. Luther comments, "Since Baptism is a divine act in which God Himself participates and since it is attended by the three exalted Persons of the Godhead, it must be prized and honored. One must agree that Baptism was not invented by any man but was instituted by God. It is not plain water but has God's Word in it and with it; and this transforms such water into a soul bath and into a bath of rejuvenation."[3] The restoration of a person in both soul and body occurs all in one act as the Christian

---

3. Luther, *Luther's Works*, Vol. 22, 174.

joined to the resurrection of Christ finds life in the One who is the Resurrection and the Life. Schmemann offers more:

> The Baptism of Christ in Jordan was the first epiphany of the Trinity in the cosmos, the manifestation of the Father, the Son, and Holy Spirit. To be redeemed, therefore, is to receive this revelation, to *know* the Trinity, to be in communion with the Triune God.[4]

That makes Jesus' Baptism a signpost and a boundary line. As you encounter a sign on the side of the road informing that you are about to cross a state line, Jesus is marking a point. From this point forward, Jesus will carry the new creation with Him wherever He goes. The essence of God's good work in the creation of the world has been distilled into the person of His Son. Where Jesus is present, so too is re-creation of broken people and a broken world. Schmemann continues, "Baptism is not a magical act adding some supernatural powers to our natural faculties. It is the beginning of life eternal itself, which unites us here in 'this world' with the 'world to come,' makes us even now in this life partakers of God's Kingdom."[5]

Everything foreshadowed in the Old Testament baptismal events has now come together. It is here that Jesus begins His public ministry. At this point Jesus begins preaching God's word to the people, formally assuming His priestly and prophetic roles. Here He begins working miracles to bring restoration and life to broken creatures, formally assuming His kingly vocation. The confirmation by the Father of Jesus' perfect righteousness is proclaimed to all who are listening. The Spirit of life signals that Jesus is already looking beyond death to new and greater life.

The Spirit shows up, not as some ghostly force or bright cloud but as a dove. Looking back to Noah and the Flood, the dove signaled the end of the baptismal work of re-creation. The dove indicated the water had done its work. Life could begin anew and Noah would soon be able to leave the ark without fear. The Bible itself adds further strength to the connection because, aside from poetic and metaphorical usages such as we find in the psalms, the only doves to be found in the entirety of Scripture are Noah's in Genesis 8 and here at Jesus' Baptism.

This seemingly minor detail expresses the scope of what God seeks to accomplish in this event. What the Flood did for creation in the past, it will do so once more through Baptism as God re-creates all of creation *beginning*

---

4. Schmemann, *Of Water and the Spirit*, 42. Italics in original.
5. Schmemann, *Of Water and the Spirit*, 42.

with mankind. With Jesus, Baptism carries all those events forward and focuses them on one point there in the Jordan. Jesus connects the Flood with His own time, while simultaneously bringing us into that event through our own Baptism. Our own reception of the Spirit in Baptism tells us God's re-creating work in our lives is nearly complete. Soon the time of death will be at an end and our life will be able to continue onward without fear.

God's re-creative activity is bound to His Word in the water. All who enter the water with the promise of God attached to it find the same result. The triune God is present and begins His restorative work on His broken creature. The Father brought the world into being through His Son, the Word. John reminds us, "All things were made through Him, and without Him was not any thing made that was made" (John 1:3). Christ proves He is the fulfillment of all that has come before, to which John the Baptist testifies, because He will be the place where this new creation comes into being. The universe was made through the Word and the Word will once again be the means through which the Father will remake His people and the world entire.

John the Baptist's statement comparing his own baptismal work with that of Christ's puts things into perspective. John's baptizing could never bring grace and forgiveness because Baptism had not yet found the focus of its action. Like the ceremonial washings at the temple, John's Baptism would function as an object lesson, teaching people what Jesus would later do. John baptizes with water. Jesus baptizes with fire and with the Holy Spirit. Jesus receives His Baptism in the water. When He returns, He will carry out the world's Baptism in fire and the Spirit. This is the eschatological fulfillment of Baptism, cleansing the world fully and finally from all taint of sin. Like the ark protected its passengers, the Holy Spirit protects those who cling to Him and have nothing to fear from the world's remaking.

Jesus' Baptism marks a transition. Up until now, God's use of water was primarily to bring about repentance. John refers to his own work by saying, "I baptize you with water for repentance" (Matt. 3:11). John could not forgive sins on his own authority, nor could he make the water anything more than water. John prepared the way for Christ's work by calling on the people to repent so God's grace would be ready and waiting. Jesus comes to the Jordan to be baptized and infuses the baptismal waters with His own divine promise. The believers in Acts 19 had repented in John's Baptism, but it would be the grace that comes through the waters connected with Christ that would bring forgiveness. Tertullian remarks here:

> And so "the baptism of repentance" was dealt with as if it were a candidate for the remission and sanctification shortly about to follow in Christ: for in that John used to preach "baptism *for* the remission of sins," the declaration was made with reference to *future* remission; if it be true, (as it is,) that repentance is antecedent, remission subsequent; and this is "preparing the way."[6]

Christ's presence has made the water into something new. It is still water, yet now it is water that carries God's promise and thus God's authority to forgive sins and everything that flows from that forgiveness.

Certain elements in the liturgical life of Israel were given the power to make other things holy. As we have seen, God gave the anointing oil this express purpose (Ex. 30:29). God later declares in Leviticus 20, "You shall be holy to Me, for I the Lord am holy and have separated you from the peoples, that you should be Mine" (v. 26). The water comes into contact with God's intrinsic holiness in the Jordan River and is, itself, made holy. So now, any time God's triune name is placed on water, His holiness comes with it and is given to the one who receives that water and that name. What was once a Baptism of repentance now carries God's holiness and grace. This leads us to no longer practice a Baptism of *repentance,* for now we confess in the Nicene Creed "one Baptism for the *remission* of sins" (emphasis added). Luther further adds:

> Note the distinction, then: Baptism is a very different thing from all other water, not by virtue of the natural substance but because here something nobler is added, for God himself stakes his honor, his power, and his might on it. Therefore it is not simply a natural water, but a divine, heavenly, holy, and blessed water—praise it in any other terms you can—all by virtue of the Word, which is a heavenly, holy Word that no one can sufficiently extol, for it contains and conveys all that is God's (LC IV).[7]

Through the Baptism of Christ, God has made the water His own and placed His name on it. He has made it into a suitable vehicle for His grace, to bring remission of sins and God's own holiness to His people so that they made be made holy like Him.

Though not directly related to His Baptism, the image of Christ on the cross in John 19:34 addresses this concept as well. Jesus becomes the Anointed One in His Baptism, carrying the burden of the world's sins to

---

6. Tertullian, "On Baptism," 674. Italics in original.
7. Kolb et al., *The Book of Concord*, 459.

their ultimate destination. On the cross, those sins are paid for. In a sense, this makes Jesus into a water purifier, taking the taint of sin on Himself. He removes that tainted water with His death on the cross. Now, as the soldier pierces His side, the water that comes out is pure and clean. His death makes the water ready and effective for our own Baptism.

This scene presents an explicit linking of Baptism and Communion, both of which find the ultimate source for their effect and use in the cross. Though these sacraments are aimed at different things, they both originate in the work of Christ. Our cleansing is made perfect in Christ, and through Him our death is accomplished so that we may rise again with Him.

8

Baptism: The Sacrament of the Spirit

JOHN 3 HAS JESUS Himself explaining some of the nuances of Baptism. Nicodemus struggled to understand what Baptism is meant to accomplish and how it does so. His confusion seems reasonable, given what Jesus was telling him. However, Jesus did not seem to think this should be confusing at all. As a Pharisee, Nicodemus had been steeped in Scripture much more than most. He certainly knew the Books of Moses and all the Levitical laws. All the baptismal events of the Old Testament were well known to him. There was no reason for him to not see what God was doing, what He was pointing them toward. The idea you might need to be born again should not have been a new one. This is what God had done for His people in each of these Old Testament events.

Jesus explained the Spirit's role in the process. Our natural birth is a birth according to the flesh. Each of us comes into being in the natural way, such as men and women have done since the days of Adam and Eve's very first children. Unfortunately, that birth carries with it the same taint and corruption of sin that our first parents brought into the world. It is a birth that brings life in the same manner every one of our parents has lived. It is a life that leads to death.

But, Adam was not born this way. Adam was not born of the flesh, but of the *Spirit*. God breathed His Spirit into Adam's unmoving clay and he became a living creature. It is this original birth, this birth brought about by the Father's workmanship and the life-giving Spirit, that carried no taint of sin. God created perfection.

Baptism: The Sacrament of the Spirit

To be free of sin's corruption, one simply needs to be born again. This concept confused Nicodemus because it is impossible for us to do or even conceive of how it might happen. Jesus told Nicodemus that it happens essentially the same way it happened for Adam: God creates you and the Spirit breathes life into you. You become a new person. Luther comments:

> The Christian message informs us that, to begin with, we must become wholly different persons, that is, that we must be born anew. But how does this happen? By the Holy Spirit and by water (John 3:5). After I have been reborn and have become pious and God-fearing, then I go forth; and everything I do in that regenerate state is good.[1]

The person you are when you are born to your parents is not the person you are when you are born of the Spirit. You may look similar. You may have the same voice, the same hobbies, the same talents and skills, you may know all the same things the previous "you" did, but you will be two entirely different people. You came into being in two completely different ways. Luther continues:

> Therefore Christ says to Nicodemus: "I have come to proclaim a different doctrine, namely, how you must be reborn to become good. To be sure, Holy Writ has contained and defined this proclamation all along, but you do not read it. Even if you do, you fail to understand the message that you must be born anew before you can perform good works. For sinners beget none but sinners; the person is corrupt." In Matt. 7:17 and 16 the Lord declares: "A bad tree can bear no good fruit; thistles do not bear figs, nor thorns grapes."[2]

This Baptism is not a superficial washing. It is a complete rebirth. It is how God restores the very thing that gives you *life*.

In the Lutheran Church, we hold Baptism in the highest regard whenever it comes up in discussion. We teach it as a sacred gift from God. However, actual practice becomes another matter. It is true when baptizing adults and even more so when baptizing infants. No outward change occurs and so we operate as if nothing has changed. It becomes no more than a certificate acknowledging the completion of a training course. You can say you did it, and it has no more impact in your life. This might not be the case if Baptism and the scope of God's work in the Sacrament were brought to

---

1. Luther, *Luther's Works, Vol. 22*, 280.
2. Luther, *Luther's Works, Vol. 22*, 280-81.

mind more often. A large part of that problem is due to our liturgical usage of Baptism, which we will examine a bit later. The other part is how we understand Baptism to operate.

God has expounded on the Spirit's role in bringing new life more than once. God speaks through the prophet Ezekiel to His people:

> I will sprinkle clean water on you, and you shall be clean from all your uncleannesses, and from all your idols I will cleanse you. And I will give you a new heart, and a new spirit I will put within you. And I will remove the heart of stone from your flesh and give you a heart of flesh. And I will put My Spirit within you, and cause you to walk in My statutes and be careful to obey My rules. (Ez. 36:25–27)

God comes to the people upon whom He has set His holy name. They have profaned His name, and so He sets about restoring the holiness His name is meant to bear. This comes about by a restorative washing, as well as a new heart and the impartation of God's Spirit. The goal of all this is then "You shall dwell in the land that I gave to your fathers, and you shall be My people, and I will be your God" (Ez. 36:28). God returns the people to the relationship they once had with Him, a relationship only possible through this baptismal washing.

King David says much the same thing in Psalm 51:

> Purge me with hyssop, and I shall be clean; wash me, and I shall be whiter than snow. Let me hear joy and gladness; let the bones that You have broken rejoice. Hide Your face from my sins, and blot out all my iniquities. Create in me a clean heart, O God, and renew a right spirit within me. Cast me not away from Your presence, and take not Your Holy Spirit from me. Restore to me the joy of Your salvation, and uphold me with a willing spirit. (Ps. 51:7–12)

Again we find the need for God to wash and make clean. Again we see the need for God to grant His Spirit and new life. All this restorative work is necessary because the natural consequence of this spiritual uncleanness is to be cast out from God's presence. As Moses told us previously, it is that presence that defines us as God's people. Without God, we become nothing at all.

While it is fine to say sin is the crux of the problem Jesus is talking about in John 3, forgiveness is not the language He is using. In fact, sin and forgiveness are not words that appear anywhere in the chapter. Choosing to see Baptism as solely about justification is to aim Jesus' words at too narrow a target and thereby lose much of the impact of what Baptism accomplishes. After all, what need would there be to dwell on the forgiveness given in Baptism when the forgiveness given through Confession and Absolution is a more regular and visible part of the church's worship life? Thankfully, Absolution and Baptism are not the same. God offers the same forgiveness through both but has given Baptism its own, unique place and purpose. The way in which God continues to work righteousness and holiness through Baptism means that the sacrament has a critical role in the life of the Christian.

Jesus' eschatological Baptism in fire that breaks the world down into its constituent parts will also break our dead and decayed bodies down so they can be remade and rise again to new life. Baptism, and the rebirth we experience there, gives us the Spirit to receive that body once again. Like breathing in stale air, we walk around day after day slowly dying because that which is within us and which is meant to animate our bodies cannot sustain us. Here in Baptism, God breathes in the fresh air of His life-giving Spirit. Luther describes Christ's message to Nicodemus by saying, "Come to Me and be baptized with water and the Holy Spirit, a Baptism that will give you a new birth and transform you into new persons, that will cause a regeneration or a renewal of your being. For the Holy Spirit works faith in us, and through this faith we regain the image of God which we lost in Paradise."[3]

Since the image of God was never about outward appearances, this rebirth can and does restore that image to us. With the Spirit in us enlivening us, with Christ's life and work around us, we truly live as God created us to be. Nicodemus was confused by how this is possible, but Jesus speaks as one who was there at the beginning and caused it to happen the first time. If the Creator was able to make mankind and the rest of the universe from nothing and cause us to live, if He can bring a flood and yet save a small group or lead an entire nation through a sea, this rebirth will not be difficult for Him.

It is at this point we must explore more deeply the involvement of the Holy Spirit within the Sacrament of Baptism. It should be noted that, in the eight or so verses of John 3 where Jesus is specifically discussing Baptism, He does not refer to Himself at all in connection with it. He directs Nicodemus's attention to the Spirit and what He does in Baptism. Certainly we know Jesus is involved in Baptism. We hear how we are connected to Him in Paul's words and in Jesus' own Baptism. But that isn't the emphasis here.

---

3. Luther, *Luther's Works*, Vol. 22, 285.

The Spirit takes center stage, which is why Baptism can be rightly thought of as the Sacrament of the Spirit.

There are a number of Christian churches that draw on passages such as 1 Corinthians 12, where the gifts of the Spirit are enumerated by Paul. The thought is generally that with Baptism comes these spiritual gifts (χαρίσματα): gifts of speaking in tongues, interpretation, miracle working, and so forth. Jesus does not describe any of those things here. He does not make any lists. Instead, as Jesus describes it, Baptism gives you one thing, and that one thing makes all the difference. Schmemann points out the overlooked detail, "It is precisely because the newness and the radical uniqueness of this sacrament is that it bestows on man not any particular gift or gifts of the Holy Spirit, *but the Holy Spirit Himself as gift* (δωρεά)."[4]

Since the typical assumption is that Baptism is just a fancy vehicle for forgiveness, and the eternal life that somehow comes about by being forgiven, the Spirit's role in Baptism becomes rather ambiguous. The Spirit is often described as bringing faith to the baptized. While faith can certainly be said to be a portion of the restorative process that Baptism carries with it, faith itself is not part of the language or themes connected with Baptism. We can easily infer that faith is built up and strengthened within the process of Baptism, since this naturally follows from a restoration of our righteousness and the image of God in Christ, but the initial creation of faith is not the goal of Baptism.

To leave the work of Baptism at simply "forgiveness of sins" thus undermines the much larger activity God accomplishes because of that forgiveness in Baptism. The rebirth that takes place through the work of the Spirit does much more than just bring life. In Luke 11, Jesus describes the work of Satan and evil spirits. He explains that driving an evil spirit out makes little difference if nothing good replaces it. While it is true that faith in Christ saves without anything being added to it, the daily work of the Spirit in Baptism further reinforces what faith has already given. Intentionally setting up the Spirit as Lord and Master of one's heart erects a barrier against Satan and warns him he is not welcome here. Luther comments on the need for sponsors to take seriously their role in Baptism:

> Therefore, you have to realize that it is no joke at all to take action against the devil and not only to drive him away from the little child but also to hang around the child's neck such a mighty, lifelong enemy. Thus it is extremely necessary to stand by the poor

---

4. Schmemann, *Of Water and the Spirit*, 79. Italics in original.

child with all your heart and with a strong faith and to plead with great devotion that God, in accordance with these prayers, would not only free the child from the devil's power but also strengthen the child, so that the child might resist him valiantly in life and in death.[5]

Baptism becomes the place where the Spirit stakes His claim over the life of the one brought to the waters. He alone rules here, not our own corrupt nature and not some deceitful demon.[6] Luther even includes in his baptismal rite the baptizer saying, "Depart, you unclean spirit, and make room for the Holy Spirit."[7] The more common Lutheran and Catholic rites in use today still include a renunciation of Satan, something only possible through the guidance and strength of the Spirit. Schmemann explains this as well:

> In the baptismal rite, which is an act of liberation and victory, the exorcisms come first because on our path to the baptismal font we unavoidably "hit" the dark and powerful figure that obstructs this path. It must be removed, chased away, if we are to proceed. The moment that the celebrant's hand has touched the head of a child of God and marked it with the sign of Christ, the Devil is there defending that which he has stolen from God and claims as his possession.[8]

This tells us one of the primary purposes of Baptism is as a defense against the assaults of Satan. The baptismal waters serve as a shield against Satan in an eschatological sense, protecting us from tumbling headlong into the darkness of sin to our own condemnation. They also defend us in the temporal sense, with the Spirit being in residence and ready to close the door whenever Satan comes knocking. This is not to say Baptism prevents a Christian from falling away from the faith, but it does indicate it is more difficult to do so. With the Spirit dwelling in one who has been baptized, the would-be apostate must then evict his resident if he wishes to be free from

---

5. Kolb et al., *The Book of Concord*, 372.

6. Some denominations claim Baptism is nothing more than our own public declaration of faith. It is we who sign on the dotted line telling the world about our faith. Yet, the work carried out in this instance cannot be done by us. We have no power to resist Satan and are powerless before him. The only claiming done is by the Spirit who takes ownership of us, body and soul, that His life might animate us into eternity.

7. Kolb et al., *The Book of Concord*, 373.

8. Schmemann, *Of Water and the Spirit*, 23–24.

God's grace. This must require a more intense and sustained effort, as God only withdraws His presence with great reluctance.

One further area where we see the Spirit at work as God brings together many of these ideas is in the events of John 7. The chapter begins with the celebration of the Feast of Booths. Jesus spends a few days teaching the crowds at the temple. Most notable about this event is what happens on the last day of the Feast, as Jesus announces that those who may come to Him and drink and those who believe in Him will have rivers of living water. John goes on to tell us Jesus is talking about the Spirit.

The connection of water and the Spirit should already catch our attention, especially when the Spirit is the one that provides eternal life. The setting for Jesus' speech gives us more to work with. The Feast of Booths recalled the Israelites' time in the wilderness, a time that we have already established was baptismal in nature. Beyond that, the text tells us Jesus gives this speech on the last day of the Feast, the day of the holy convocation. This might not garner much attention except that Leviticus 23 tells us this day is the eighth day of the feast and thus alludes to the larger body of eighth day theology.

Jesus intentionally draws these various baptismal strands and weaves them together in a way that tells us the work of the Spirit in the lives of believers cannot be overstated. Luther comments on the passage by saying, "Although Christ did not explain the terms 'rivers' and 'living water,' they pertain to the Holy Spirit. Those who possess the Gospel and have received the Holy Spirit can comfort, instruct, teach, warn, yes, serve the entire world and help destroy death and gain eternal life."[9]

We also find the prophecy of Zechariah 13 as a tributary to this as well: "On that day there shall be a fountain opened for the house of David and the inhabitants of Jerusalem, to cleanse them from sin and uncleanness." Luther shares his thoughts on this particular passage:

> This fountain might well and properly be understood as referring to Baptism, in which the Spirit is given and all sins are washed away. But because of the quarrelsome factions, who despise Baptism and ridicule everything that points to Baptism, we shall drop that too and cling to the fact that Christ, in John 4:14, speaks of a spring of living water—and this the evangelist himself interprets as being the Spirit, whom they are to receive who believe in Him

---

9. Luther, *Luther's Works*, Vol. 23, 277.

(John 7:38 f.). This spring is now open to all Christians, and it washes away two kinds of filth; sin and uncleanness.[10]

The prophecy is given life in the form of Christ and His gift of the Spirit through the waters of Baptism. The water that flows in Baptism cleanses us inside and out. This is what allows Paul to say, "But you were washed, you were sanctified, you were justified in the name of the Lord Jesus Christ and by the Spirit of our God" (1 Cor. 6:11). The Spirit's work is comprehensive and all-encompassing.

The presence of the Spirit relates back to Genesis, both at creation and the Flood. We have already seen the connection the Spirit makes to the Flood through the use of the dove. Jesus' words in John 3 speak of rebirth. The presence of the dove at the Flood and here at Jesus' Baptism indicates the world itself was reborn in the waters of the Flood. Re-creation tells us the world was made new. Rebirth tells us it does not simply exist—creation *lives*. This is not to be taken in the sense of a pervasive earth spirit, such as Gaia or Mother Nature, but rather that God's world is not made new to be barren and lifeless. God's creation was meant to hold abundant life. The work of the Spirit tells us we are united to the Flood and the re-creation and rebirth of the world through Jesus' own Baptism. His Baptism becomes the bridge where the Old and New Testament ages connect. We are able to be reborn through Him. Through Christ all things were made and so through Christ all things are remade. The Spirit gave life to the first people and so the Spirit gives life to us once again. Luther connects this idea in his commentary on John 15:

> When I am baptized or converted by the Gospel, the Holy Spirit is present. He takes me as clay and makes of me a new creature, which is endowed with a different mind, heart, and thoughts, that is, with a true knowledge of God and a sincere trust in His grace. To summarize, the very essence of my heart is renewed and changed. This makes me a new plant, one that is grafted on Christ the Vine and grows from Him. My holiness, righteousness, and purity do not stem from me, nor do they depend on me. They come solely from Christ and are based only in Him, in whom I am rooted by faith, just as the sap flows from the stalk into the branches. Now I am like Him and of His kind. Both He and I are of one nature and essence, and I bear fruit in Him and through Him. This fruit is not mine; it is the Vine's.[11]

---

10. Luther, *Luther's Works, Vol. 20*, 331.
11. Luther, *Luther's Works, Vol. 24*, 226.

Past and present flow together in the waters of the Jordan and, because that connection is established in Christ, it exists eternally. This makes the very waters of the Jordan flow to every font and pool where Christians encounter the triune God to find their rebirth in the water and the Spirit.

The work of the Spirit in Baptism makes possible the special goal of Jesus' Baptism. Where all Old Testament themes are signs for what is to come, Jesus' Baptism marks the reality. Jesus brings to fulfillment all of these events, both major and minor, collecting the various tributaries into one flowing river, bringing new life to all who enter it. Jesus melds the past and present together as one. Moses, Noah, Adam, and all of the others who participated in some way in the preparatory imagery of Baptism now see the work fulfilled in Christ. The present is brought into the past through God's re-creative work and the past is brought into the present as Baptism is made into reality.

9

Baptism: The Sacrament of Discipleship

As Jesus' earthly ministry came to a close, He left His disciples with a task. "All authority in heaven and on earth has been given to Me. Go therefore and make disciples of all nations, baptizing them in the name of the Father and of the Son and of the Holy Spirit, teaching them to observe all that I have commanded you" (Matt. 28:18–20). While Baptism had been going on in various forms for a while now, from the ritual washings in temple worship to John the Baptist's Baptism of repentance, now we have a direct command from God to continue baptizing. Not only do we have God's command but Jesus tells us the new form that Baptism is to take.

The inclusion of the trinitarian name focuses our attention on something new and radical that is being added to what would otherwise be a meaningful but mundane act. The name serves to differentiate this ritual washing from all others. Here Baptism truly becomes holy. The water of Baptism is set apart for use by the triune God alone. Man no longer has ownership over this water and cannot define how it should be used. God claims the water's use in conveying His grace and life to the believer. Any other use becomes a denigration of what God has instituted. As Christ holds the authority to make this command, nothing we do may contradict it.

One discussion of this is found in Luther's Marburg Articles: "Ninth, that holy baptism is a sacrament which has been instituted by God as an aid to such a faith, and because God's command, 'Go, baptize' [cf. Matt. 28:19], and God's promise, 'He who believes' [Mark 16:16], are connected with it, it is therefore not merely an empty sign or watchword among Christians but, rather, a sign and work of God by which our faith grows and through which we are regenerated to [eternal] life."[1] There are many in the church who see Baptism as being devoid of grace, of being empty of benefit. They see it as being a superficial work of man that only has meaning within the context of that particular congregation. This completely dismisses the work of the Spirit and makes the washing "Baptism" in name only. This misappropriation of God's holy things can only bring negative temporal, and even eternal, consequences.

> Others treat Baptism as simply a point at which they receive a temporary infusion of the Spirit. This means when faith seems to wane, the reason must be that the Spirit's influence has also waned, and the solution is the Christian must be baptized again to reignite the flame of faith. Aside from the lack of biblical support for rebaptizing in general, the deeper issue is the complete lack of understanding of what the Spirit is doing, turning eternal blessings into temporary spiritual boosts.[2]

The triune name binds the creative work of God—Father, Son, and Holy Spirit—to the activity taking place within the waters. The triune God created the world and mankind. Now the triune God re-creates and makes new. Though we can say no work of God is truly compartmentalized to just one or two of the persons of the Trinity, for all participate in one way or another, here the work is made quite explicit. The Father reshapes our being into that which we once had. The Father uses His own Son as the spiritual mold. Our Baptism conforms us to Christ so that our life more and more begins to resemble His. We become like Him. The more we are immersed in His grace, the more we begin to think and act like Christ Himself, never seeking to reach beyond ourselves but modeling ourselves on the one example of perfect righteousness that exists. Finally, we are enlivened by the Spirit to follow in Christ's footsteps as we journey through the grave into the light of eternal day.

---

1. Luther, *Luther's Works*, Vol. 38, 87.

2. Luther speaks at length about the incongruity of rebaptizing, such that I have little to add to his discourse. One small excerpt is, "For if an Anabaptist hears (that is, if he does not want to be obstinate but teachable) that just as John believed and was made holy when Christ came and spoke through the mouth of his mother, so a child becomes a believer if Christ in baptism speaks to him through the mouth of the one who baptizes, since it is his Word, his commandment, and his word cannot be without fruit, then the Anabaptist must admit that it may be so, that he cannot altogether and firmly deny it, nor cite any Scripture to the contrary."
Luther, *Luther's Works*, Vol. 40, 245–46.

Baptism: The Sacrament of Discipleship

The triune name functions as a sign and seal of whose you are. Luther offers, "To be baptized in God's name is to be baptized not by human beings but by God Himself. Although it is performed by human hands, it is nevertheless truly God's own act" (LC IV).[3] God's name serves the same purpose as the rainbow after the Flood. He puts His name on you to serve as a sign you are one of His children. The judgment that will fall on the world will pass you by. You are not a stranger to Him. The trinitarian work of God comes together as the Spirit lives in you, Christ is all around you, and the Father sees you and claims you as His own. The baptisms some churches do that are in the name of Christ alone or some variation, aside from simply running contrary to Christ's own command, fail to grasp the magnitude of what God accomplishes and the significance of the Trinity's involvement in the Sacrament.

The use of the trinitarian name is only one item of significance in Jesus' command. The larger duty Jesus entrusts the disciples with is to make more disciples. He indicates two items that are necessary in the making of disciples: teaching and baptizing. Both are aspects of Christian life the church must continuously fight to uphold. Many in the church see no need for further education and think the bare minimum understanding of God and His grace is all that is necessary. They relegate their confirmation teachings to a bit of theological trivia and spend little time considering how to embody Christ and to carry that grace to the world, in large part because they have so little to work with.

Even for those who accept the importance of teaching, Baptism is still a requirement if one seeks to truly fulfill the role of disciple. With a fuller understanding of Baptism, the reasoning for this becomes quite clear. To be a disciple does not mean offering a simple vow to follow Jesus. It does not mean being dedicated to the Christian faith. It does not mean being a member of a local congregation or holding to a specific set of beliefs. All of those may be part of what a disciple does, but they are not who a disciple *is*.

Jesus stipulates teaching and Baptism as the two requirements for the role of disciple. It is unfortunate that *apostle* and *disciple* tend to be used interchangeably in the church. We typically use the words to refer to the men involved in the life of Christ in the New Testament, and because they are referred to by both words, the meanings become blurred. But they are not the same thing. They denote two different roles. Both roles are a part of Christian life, but they work differently.

---

3. Kolb et al., *The Book of Concord*, 457.

One place where we can see the two words at work is in Mark 6. Mark 6:7 tells us Jesus sends the Twelve out in pairs to proclaim the Gospel and He gives them the authority to heal and exorcise. There is an interlude dealing with the death of John the Baptist. Then, in Mark 6:30, the Twelve return. They are referred to here as apostles. This stands to reason as *apostle* means "one who is sent." A few verses later, in Mark 6:35, the Twelve are referred to as "disciples," and that is the word that continues to be used for them from that point forward. Those who had been sent and carried out the duties of an apostle have now returned to their Teacher and Lord, where they resume the role of disciple.

Discipleship is characterized by this attitude toward God. Sitting at the feet of one's Lord to humbly receive whatever He chooses to give is the fundamental posture of discipleship. That means whatever the Lord gives is welcomed: His grace, His leadership, and His teachings. The Twelve are referred to as disciples through the life of Christ because that is their primary role during that time. They follow their Teacher and Lord everywhere He goes, and they learn everything He has to teach, not just in terms of verbal instruction but as the perfect example of righteousness. They learn what it means to live the perfect life. They may not be able to attain it, but having that example gives them an idea what they should be seeking to emulate.

This explains why Jesus denotes teaching as fundamental to discipleship. Baptism as a requirement might seem a little more confusing, but with the background established from the Old Testament and Jesus' own words, the answer presents itself. Without the rebirth brought by the Spirit and the re-creation into the image and likeness of Christ, the teaching given will only get you so far. Having God's teaching does not enable you to carry out that teaching, any more than knowing the Ten Commandments enables you to keep them. For this to be a possibility, God must work in you and through you to empower you to live out what you have learned.

This is not to say a Christian who lives without Baptism lives outside God's salvation. Everyone in the Old Testament lived before the fulfillment of Baptism and many in the New Testament, such as the thief on the cross who confessed his faith, lived without Baptism and were still saved. Nevertheless, now that Baptism has been given to us, those who continue living without it will live without one of the greatest gifts God wishes to give His people. Their lives will be incomplete and stunted. God's re-creative work will have to await them on the Last Day, instead of beginning in their lives when they receive His Name at the font.

Baptism: The Sacrament of Discipleship

Christians who have come to the font and who have received scriptural teaching are living out lives of true discipleship. This is a fundamental part of Christian identity. Their Baptism continues God's re-creating process throughout their lives as the Spirit continues to give them life. The teaching becomes lifelong as well. Every day, their lives are being conformed ever closer to that of Christ's own life. Every day, the Spirit breathes eternal life into their broken bodies. Every day, a disciple thirsts for what Christ gives, in order to learn and grow into the Christian God has formed us to be.

Even in a state of perfect righteousness, the role of discipleship is intrinsic to who we are and is bound up with our very identity. Adam lived as a perfect disciple before the Fall. Luther observes this:

> And so when Adam had been created in such a way that he was, as it were, intoxicated with rejoicing toward God and was delighted also with all the other creatures, there is now created a new tree for the distinguishing of good and evil, so that Adam might have a definite way to express his worship and reverence toward God. After everything had been entrusted to him to make use of it according to his will, whether he wished to do so for necessity or for pleasure, God finally demands from Adam that at this tree of the knowledge of good and evil he demonstrate his reverence and obedience toward God and that he maintain this practice, as it were, of worshiping God by not eating anything from it.[4]

Adam had a focus to his life: the tree of the knowledge of good and evil. It is especially true of Eve's case that her failure was first and foremost one of discipleship. Had she gone to her Teacher and Lord when Satan questioned His command, instead of deciding she knew better, she would have avoided the temptation. Jesus tells the Twelve, "A disciple is not above his teacher, nor a servant above his master. It is enough for the disciple to be like his teacher, and the servant like his master" (Matt. 10:24–25). Adam and Eve acted with the assumption they knew better than God Himself, and it brought death into the world.

A disciple learns at the feet of his master, humble and receptive. A disciple is baptized so that she may carry out what she has learned. Both are necessary. A disciple who chooses not to learn any more is telling the Teacher He has nothing further to teach. A disciple who chooses not to be baptized is telling the Teacher he is capable of carrying out everything he has learned without any assistance.

---

4. Luther, *Luther's Works*, Vol. 1, 94.

Even in righteousness, discipleship was a part of the life of the believer. The God who continues to create wonders always has something new to teach and to show. God baptizes His people with water to bring them back to that state of righteousness. Christ, who undoes the sin of Adam by correcting it in His own life, brings us back to the time before that sin so that we can be disciples once again. The vocations given back to us as we are restored to the image of God—those of prophet, priest, and king—are all carried out under the aegis of discipleship. We are kings, but we are kings who bow to He who is rightly called King of kings and Lord of lords. We are priests, but priests whose purpose is bound up in service to God. We are prophets, but our gift of prophecy and the words we proclaim are given to us. They are not something we are able to do on our own.

Jesus as the Second Adam, as the one who is meant to relive Adam's life in a state of righteousness rather than sin, is reinforced by the context of His own Baptism. Directly following Jesus' Baptism, He goes out into the wilderness to fast. Following this, while He is physically weak, He is confronted by Satan and his lies. Where Adam succumbed in the garden, Jesus fights back with God's own promises and stands triumphant. Jesus relives that initial conversation with Satan in Genesis 3 as it was meant to go.

This connection is further buttressed by the time period in which Jesus is fasting. Forty days in the wilderness draws our attention back to Genesis 7 once more, where God announces the rain will fall forty days and forty nights. Forty is also found in the number of years the Israelites were in the wilderness. In both cases, the forty is a time of purification, preparing the people and the world for what God was accomplishing through His grace. Both cases are also closely intertwined with the work of Baptism.

Jesus identifies the most basic attitude of any believer, that of discipleship. Grace and forgiveness are not earned but humbly received. The attitude of discipleship is necessary to know you are meant to receive and not to earn. As creatures, we will never be greater than, or even equal to, our Creator. This is why the first sin of Adam and Eve was a rejection of their role as creaturely disciple.

Had sin not entered the world, Baptism might have been unnecessary. Since sin is here and we do not have the perfect righteousness we need, we require Baptism to adopt the humbly receptive posture needed to receive God's grace and life. The saints of the Old Testament looked forward to that restoration even as they participated in the various prefiguring events God brought. The baptismal work of the Old Testament re-created people

Baptism: The Sacrament of Discipleship

so that they could resume their life as disciples. A Christian who continues to hold this humble attitude continues to receive life from the Spirit and righteousness in Christ. He continues to listen to Christ as his Teacher and Lord and seeks to emulate Him to the best of his ability. A Christian who no longer desires to do these things has thrown off her position as disciple and rejects everything God seeks to give through it.

Baptism is considered the rite and sacrament that binds a Christian to the people of God. The trinitarian life that marks every facet of his being—the re-creation that has taken place—is one indication God has claimed a person as His own. In addition to this is the illustration and example given by each of the Old Testament threads that connect to Baptism. In each, the faith held by the Christian goes from passive to active. In each instance, the faith of those involved changes from a simple trust in God to provide and becomes involved in God's specific and personal assurance of salvation. In Baptism, the Spirit refines the immature faith of the Christian and allows it to bloom and come to life.

The Spirit is already present in someone who has faith, for Paul says in 1 Corinthians 12 "Therefore I want you to understand that no one speaking in the Spirit of God ever says 'Jesus is accursed!' and no one can say 'Jesus is Lord' except in the Holy Spirit" (v. 3). Now the Spirit takes that seed and helps it to grow and flourish. Before Baptism a person can rightly be called a Christian on account of their faith. Now, through the work of the Spirit in the living waters of Baptism, a Christian is actually *living out* that faith.

The entire time the Israelites wandered in the wilderness became one long lesson on discipleship. If the Israelites stopped trusting in God, they perished. Having been baptized in the Red Sea and the Jorden, they lived out that faith before the world as they, quite literally, followed God around wherever He led them. They put their trust in Him to lead them out of Egypt. Now they learned to live out that trust and to actually be the people of God in deed and not just name.

Beginning with the awareness that Baptism, and everything that comes with it, is a gift, not earned but graciously given from Teacher to disciple, the would-be disciple comes to the font where He is claimed by the Teacher. One cannot declare himself to be a disciple. That would imply the person has the authority to make such a decision. Only the Teacher can choose who follows Him. Jesus explains this Himself in the sacramental context of John 6: "No one can come to Me unless the Father who sent Me draws him" (v. 43).

10

Baptism: The Sacrament of Worship Restored

THE THEMES OF BAPTISM pervade all of Scripture from the very beginning to the very end. For Baptism to show up in so many places and in such important events gives us an indication how important Baptism is meant to be in the life of the church. Thus far, we have examined many different themes and seen how they all flow together. This list is not exhaustive, though it does include all the events that most strongly influence our understanding of baptismal theology.

Other Scriptural events that are linked to Baptism tend to be more illustrative, rather than foundational for theology. Events surrounding the Jordan particularly fall into this category, such as Elijah striking the water with his cloak to walk across on dry ground (2 Ki. 2) or Elisha causing the axe head to float (2 Ki. 3). That is not to say these passages have no place in a discussion of Baptism but merely that they do not add a great deal to our understanding of what Baptism does.

Given that Baptism restores our prophetic, priestly, and kingly vocations—as well as the vocation of disciple, which undergirds the rest—it also marks the point at which true worship can begin. The Christian who has put on Christ now properly reflects God. That which has been freely given by God and received in trust and faith is now returned to God through sacrificial offerings of praise, worship, and care for one's neighbor.

This also means Baptism is the point at which the Christian, now re-created and enlivened by the work of Christ and the Spirit, has the ability to begin living out the life of Christ. Since our Baptism links us not just to Christ's death but also His resurrection and life, it is only natural that Baptism be the foundation for the life of the church. To be sure, the Eucharist will be an even greater expression of the church-in-Christ, but the Eucharist functions within the context of Baptism and is built on that foundation. The Eucharist cannot properly operate outside of that context.

With a strong theological foundation on the purpose and effects of Baptism, the question must then be asked, "What do I do with this?" Thus far the discussion has revolved around how Baptism intersects the life of the Christian and what it does there. Without some discussion of how Baptism continues to influence our life, the significance of the event fades. Baptism is meant to affect the entire life of the Christian and of the church as a whole. Schmemann highlights the serious problem that is associated with our use of Baptism today:

> Baptism is, first of all, absent from the Church's *liturgy*, if by liturgy we mean that which the term *leitourgia* has always meant: a corporate act in which the whole Church, i.e. the entire community, is involved, in which it really participates. Is it not true indeed that, from the liturgical point of view, Baptism today has become a private family celebration performed as a rule outside the corporate worship of the Church, precisely outside its *leitourgia*?[1]

With our look at the various themes of Baptism, hopefully the seriousness of the problem comes across. If Baptism is as foundational to the life of the church as Scripture makes it out to be, then it must continue to be so. With that in mind, it is worth exploring the liturgical application of Baptism and how the themes of Baptism might be better incorporated into the life of the church so the richness of the Sacrament may permeate the life of the church and of each individual Christian.

The liturgical application of Baptism can take a variety of forms. Many things have come to be associated with the baptismal rite through the ages, all seeking to expand upon one theological thread or another. That is not to say all these ritual actions are beneficial to every Christian. However, since many of them have been in use in one form or another since the very beginnings of the church, they are at least worth exploring and understanding.

Before we begin, it is important to take to heart Luther's warning:

---

1. Schmemann, *Of Water and the Spirit*, 8. Italics in original.

> Bear in mind, too, that in baptism the external ceremonies are least important, such as blowing under the eyes, making the sign of the cross, putting salt in the mouth or spit and clay in the ears and nose, anointing the breast and shoulders with oil, smearing the head with chrism, putting on the christening robe, placing a burning candle in the child's hand, and whatever else has been added by humans to embellish baptism. For certainly a baptism can occur without any of these things, and they are not the actual devices from which the devil shrinks or flees.[2]

Only the actual washing of the Christian in the name of the Trinity constitutes Baptism. Everything else is an addition to that. Those additions may be extremely useful and beneficial for the Christian and the church in comprehending what is taking place and seeing the full wonder of the mystery being given, but they must not overshadow the act of Baptism itself. Nor should these elements be thought of as indispensable if circumstances simply do not allow for them.

That said, these external elements can be helpful in bringing the theology of Baptism to life. They may not have a specific promise attached to them, but if they can support the Spirit's work in Baptism, as a buttress supports a cathedral, then the structure as a whole becomes more resilient. To that end, we will examine several rituals that have been used in conjunction with Baptism to look at the theological underpinnings as well as other ways baptismal theology might be woven into the life of the church.

LITURGICAL CONTEXT

The relationship of Baptism to the worship service has changed considerably since the earliest days of the church. No longer is Baptism only done on Easter Vigil. No longer are the recipients of Baptism primarily adults, at least in North America. The use of the Sacrament on an average Sunday has become commonplace.

The argument can certainly be made that every Sunday is a celebration of the Resurrection and so every Sunday is proper for Baptism. That is an entirely valid line of thinking and it would not do to discount the value of any Sunday in the life of the church. Each Sunday stands as a remembrance of the eighth day, and so each Sunday continues Christ's trek into eternity.

---

2. Kolb et al., *The Book of Concord*, 372.

While that is true, with Baptism joining us to Christ's life, there is something to be said for bringing that aspect of Baptism to the fore. Paul's statement connecting our Baptism to Christ's death and resurrection makes Easter still the natural choice for a Baptism. It is one thing to hear you have been baptized into Christ's death and quite another to live out that event knowing you now share the Resurrection with Christ. The other major festivals are also fine choices. Christmas and the celebration of the Incarnation takes on the added baptismal significance, though it draws on different aspects of what Baptism is doing. Christ is born into human flesh to be the Second Adam, achieving that perfect righteousness Adam gave up so that, through my Baptism, I might now receive that righteousness back again and return to the perfection that existed before the Fall. Pentecost looks instead at the gift of the Spirit. We see the Twelve on Pentecost anointed with the Spirit and empowered to live out their vocations once more, in particular their priestly and prophetic roles. Many are taught and baptized on Pentecost, as the new Christian likewise receives the Spirit in Baptism and is added to as a member of God's church. Lesser festivals might also find baptismal connections. Epiphany could be shown as God drawing all people to Himself just as He calls all people to the water where the Light of the World becomes theirs as well. The Baptism of Jesus has obvious connections as Christ establishes the means by which we may enter into His life so that His death and resurrection can be explicitly given to us. Other connections can likely be found as well; however, it is recommended that one be cautious with moving further away from these high points in Jesus' life.

The early church centered the rite of Baptism within the context of Christ's death and resurrection to make very clear part of what the Christian receives in Baptism. The more distance there is between Baptism and these clear events, the more difficult it may be for the Christian and the church to perceive their Baptism as actually bringing them into that life. This causes a great deal of the foundational theology of Baptism to never accomplish its purpose.

The context of Baptism within the worship service is also important. The progression of Christian life from faith to Baptism and then on to Communion is already clear from the themes of Baptism. To locate Baptism in the center of the service is to make explicit Baptism's role: not an individual event but a public one which joins the Christian to the larger church. As Schmemann pointed out earlier, it is tragically commonplace for baptisms to be done privately with perhaps only family and a few friends in attendance.³ He also says:

> [Modern theology] views everything in the Church—sacraments, rites, and even the Church herself—as primarily, if not exclusively, individual "means of grace," aimed at the individual, at his individual sanctification. It has lost the very categories by which to express the Church and her life as that new reality which precisely overcomes and transcends all "individualism," transforms *individuals* into *persons,* and in which men are persons only because and inasmuch as they are united to God and, in Him, to one another and to the whole of life.⁴

This not only sets a bad precedent for the Christian, reinforcing a distorted idea of his relationship with God being strictly individual, but also denies the rest of the church the ability to welcome the newly baptized into their community and rejoice at the gift God has given. It is the church that welcomes the new member into their midst and celebrates that their number has grown by one. Just as a family rejoices when a new child is born, so too does the church rejoice when a Christian is reborn.

Even within the community of the faithful, Baptism is often conducted outside of the service proper, tacked on at the beginning or at the end. This can give the impression Baptism is not an act of worship or that it is somehow disruptive to the flow of the liturgy. This reduces its status as one of the primary events of Christian life and turns it into something akin to a requirement that simply needs to be attended to and nothing more. While the circumstances of the baptismal rite are, to a certain extent, adiaphora and while we must be careful not to discount the efficacy of baptisms conducted in exigent circumstances, it is also important to recognize that the context of the rite says something to the recipient and to the church as a whole as to what is taking place here. God is always teaching His people about Himself and the work He is carrying out on their behalf. That is never more true than in His Word and sacraments, where His grace is directly intersecting the lives of the faithful. Every effort should be made to ensure

---

3. This is not to say a Baptism done in such a manner is never acceptable. Extenuating circumstances do arise that require things out of the ordinary, such as when there is an emergency and Baptism simply cannot wait for a more appropriate time. By and large, however, these are the exceptions and not the rule. Few Baptisms require these sorts of measures.

4. Schmemann, *Of Water and the Spirit*, 143. Italics in original.

the context does as much as possible to express and illuminate the work of God in and through the sacrament.

Since discipleship consists of both teaching and baptizing, the baptismal rite has typically been connected with the Apostles' Creed as a profession of the faith into which the Christian is being baptized. It is an acknowledgment that this is the God who is claiming the one who comes to the font and a declaration that this is the God the Christian will be following. This is the God who has brought me to the font to be reborn in water and the Word.

Since faith receives the blessings of God in all of the places He offers it, including Baptism, it is fitting to situate the baptismal rite within the service in place of the Creed. In that way, it comes after the Scripture readings, where the Spirit is active in kindling faith, and becomes the response of the faithful who professes that faith in the form of the Creed and hears God's call to come to the water to be re-created. Just as a child might describe his mother or father to explain who his family is, the baptized child of God describes the Triune God who has claimed him. This also places the rite before the celebration of Holy Communion. The biblical themes forming the foundation for Communion tell us it is the fulfillment of what was begun in Baptism and not the other way around.

In this way, Baptism conveys its place within Christian life as the next step beyond the simple reception of faith. This is where a Christian goes from merely being present to becoming a disciple and actively following Christ through His life, death, and resurrection. This is where God takes a more direct hand in the life of the Christian and prepares him to receive the still-greater gift of Holy Communion.

Christ's life is necessarily the church's life. As the liturgical year allows us to walk through the life of Christ and retell the story of our salvation once more, it is only natural for our Baptism to fit within that life. It is likewise natural for our Baptism to fit within the context of the worship service which serves as our foremost expression of the priestly vocation that is being given back to us.

SIGN OF THE CROSS

Few external elements are so tightly woven into the fabric of Baptism as the sign of the cross. The sign of the cross is the simplest and, at the same time, most profound external element to be found within the ritual of Baptism.

The indelible mark of the Spirit, expressed in the theology of anointing, is found within this simple ritual. Whenever the sign of the cross is made, the Christian is reminded of everything that has been given to her in Baptism.

Having put on Christ in Baptism, making the sign of the cross becomes an outward physical display of what is taking place spiritually. Like putting on the priestly ephod or the king's crown, the sign makes a declaration of who the Christian is in this world. Those coming forward to be baptized are marked with the sign of the cross as the visible mark and insignia of Christ as we put on Christ but are also claimed by Him.

The sign is a mark of ownership. Christ offers His life on the cross and the sign is both the indication of who is receiving the benefit of Christ's sacrificial death and the reality that the Christian has received God's grace because of that death. In the baptismal rite, Luther follows the sign of the cross with a prayer:

> O almighty and eternal God, Father of our Lord Jesus Christ, I call to you on behalf of this, your servant, N., who asks for the gift of your baptism and desires your eternal grace through spiritual rebirth. Receive him, Lord, and as you have said, 'Ask and you shall receive, seek and you shall find, knock and it shall be open for you,' so give now the blessing to him who asks and open the door to him who knocks on it, so that he may obtain the eternal blessing of this heavenly bath and receive the promised kingdom you give through Christ our Lord. Amen.[5]

Through faith, the Spirit has brought this Christian to the font seeking rebirth and God has heard that plea and responds. No one is deserving of the gift, but God has bound Himself by His own promise to bring the faithful into Christ's death and resurrection through the waters of Baptism. The sign marks one who should have been on the cross but was saved instead by Christ's self-given death.

Hearkening back to the covenant of the rainbow, God looks down at the one marked with the cross and knows this one will not perish in the baptismal flood. This one will not find the grave to be the end. The celebrant marks the Christian with the sign of the cross to make clear, wherever this newborn Christian was headed before, the goal and destination is now the kingdom of God. As the pillar of cloud and fire protected the Israelites through the Red Sea, now Christ protects Christians from the baptismal

---

5. Kolb et al., *The Book of Concord*, 373.

flood. He sets their minds on the destination, declaring He will lead them to the new promised land, the kingdom of God.

The sign of the cross, as a declaration of ownership, also wards off the attacks of Satan. The Spirit has taken up residence here and Satan is no longer welcome. Satan may rage at everything God does in and through Baptism, but he is powerless to affect any of it. He cannot throw out the Spirit.

Because the sign of the cross is bound to the baptismal event, it is bound also to the death and resurrection of Christ. The liturgy is replete with reminders of what Christ has done on behalf of His people. Making the sign of the cross connects Christians to their Baptism once more, bringing to mind that everything Christ has given is still theirs and will always be.

Because you are claimed by God, the sign of the cross becomes your continued assurance that you have been made righteous and holy by Him. Baptism's connection to the trinitarian name is found right in Jesus' command. This makes the sign of the cross also the mark of discipleship. God's judgment falls on the world, just as it had in the Flood. That judgment should fall on me, but I make the sign of the cross to remind both myself and the Father that I have been baptized and made righteous through the work of the Son and the Spirit. The Word has been revealed to me and I have received it in faith. I follow Christ through the power of the Spirit and continuously seek to be conformed more and more to His likeness.

Though the sign is bestowed in the baptismal rite, this ongoing effect becomes part of the liturgical life of the church. Whenever the Trinity is named, I am encouraged to make the sign of the cross to call my Baptism to mind once more. This is the God who has claimed me and made me His own.

The trinitarian invocation that begins our worship is our priestly announcement of who we are here to worship and a call for the triune God to honor His promise to be present among us. As priests who have been restored to our vocation by Baptism, we make the sign to remember that we have been made worthy to be in the holy presence of God and that we are carrying out our duty in calling Him into creation where He may be properly worshiped by us and by those around us.

Since disciples are made by teaching and baptizing, it is only appropriate that the baptismal sign be made during the Invocation which begins the liturgical Service of the Word. The Service of the Word is where we return to the feet of our Rabbi and Lord to learn again what it means to follow in His footsteps. This is where we continue our journey of discipleship as we walk behind our Master through the liturgical year to hear what He has done for us and look forward to where He is leading us. The Service of the Word is for disciples. It is the place in the liturgy where disciples are able to be what they have been called to be. The sign calls us back to where we were made clean, where we were born again.

Luther sees the sign of the cross being a part of daily life for the Christian. While the worship service is the highest expression of discipleship, the life of the disciple is one of daily following Christ. In his evening ritual he directs making the sign of the cross before praying to the triune God for protection and then continuing with the Creed, Lord's Prayer, and his Evening Prayer. The sign helps the church to see the effects of our Baptism at every moment of our lives. God's re-creative work never ceases, and the Spirit continues to defend us against the assaults of the enemy. At any point when fear or doubts assail us, we need only make the sign of the cross to know our Baptism has bound us to God through an everlasting covenant. We have already died with Him on the cross and have already entered into eternal life.

THE WHITE GARMENT

The custom of wearing a white gown or something similar as a part of the baptismal rite goes back to the very early period of the church. In the early church, the newly baptized Christians would be given white robes to wear. This allowed them to display openly the new spiritual status they possessed. The allusion to "putting on Christ" is obvious. The Christian, in some minute way, begins to resemble Christ Himself, reflecting the image of Christ in His transfiguration. The church now sees the Christian as God sees him.

The imagery also brings to bear the eschatological continuity of Baptism. The great multitude before the throne in Revelation 7 is described as those who "have washed their robes and made them white in the blood of the Lamb" (v. 14). Since one who is righteous and clean is fit to be in the presence of God, the baptized Christian can number herself among those in this passage who are welcomed and able to be in God's presence. The multitude in Revelation are carrying out the priestly role of mankind as they declare God's praises.

The white robe also recalls the linen coat the high priest was to wear on the Day of Atonement. On other days he wore all of his priestly finery as he carried out his sacerdotal duties as God's representative and mediated on behalf of God's people in a more general sense. Here on the Day of Atonement, finery becomes presumptuous. In God's gracious presence there is only the awareness that we are unworthy to be there and we abide there solely because of that grace. The baptized Christian becomes aware of this too as he approaches the font. Schmemann adds:

> Thus the rite of the white garment is not merely a reminder of and a call to a pure and righteous life, for if it were only that, it would indeed add nothing to Baptism: it is self-evident that we are baptized in order to lead a Christian life, which, in turn, must be as "pure" and "righteous" as possible. What it reveals and therefore communicates is the radical *newness* of that purity and righteousness of that *new* spiritual life for which the neophyte was regenerated in the baptismal immersion and which will now be bestowed upon him through the "seal of the gift of the Holy Spirit."[6]

Bathed in the waters of Christ's righteousness, he is anointed for priestly duty and is given the privilege, through Christ, of stepping behind the veil to see God face to face.

In modern times, infants typically wear a white baptismal gown as part of their baptismal rite. However, as was the case in the early church, the benefits are just as noteworthy for adults. In both cases, the church as a whole is able to see and celebrate the redemption given to the Christian and welcome her into God's presence.

This carries over into liturgical vestments as well. The alb or surplice typically worn by pastors and liturgical assistants recalls the priestly vestments on the Day of Atonement and are likewise baptismal in nature. It is by benefit of the pastor's Baptism that he is enabled to carry out his duties before the congregation. He fulfills his priestly duty by speaking God's Word to the assembly and bringing the sacrifices of the people before God. His Baptism is what enables him to safely approach the special and gracious presence of God that rests on the mercy seat in the body and blood of Christ.

While the pastor carries out these duties on behalf of the congregation, the baptized assembly continues to carry out these same duties in the context of their own life. This gives the white garment the same ongoing significance as Baptism, allowing the baptized to "step into" the priestly role that has been given to them in Baptism and begin living out that vocation in their daily lives.

---

6. Schmemann, *Of Water and the Spirit*, 72. Italics in original.

EXORCISM

The modernist move away from some of the more spiritual and mysterious elements of the Christian faith has caused the idea of exorcism to be glossed over in our day. While it is still present in some form in most Western and Eastern liturgies that continue to hold a deeper understanding of Baptism, what is there tends to be severely truncated.

Luther's own baptismal rite has the celebrant commanding Satan to leave to make room for the Spirit and later has the recipient verbally renounce Satan.[7] The modern Catholic rite has a prayer asking God to cast Satan out and later a similar renunciation. The modern Lutheran rite has, sadly, dropped the exorcism, leaving only a renunciation. While it is possible to go overboard in our emphasis on Satan's influence, it is also possible to allow our modernist sensibilities to rule the day, such that this important aspect of Baptism ends up being left out.

The exorcism is not meant to simply be a request. It is a command based on the promise of the Spirit to take up residence within our hearts. Schmemann explains further:

> What is of paramount importance for us, however, is that the Church has always had the experience of the demonic, has always, in plain words, *known the Devil*... We *speak* to the Devil! It is here that the Christian understanding of the *word* as, above all, *power* is made manifest. In the desacralized and secularized worldview of the "modern man," speech, as everything else, has been "devaluated," reduced to its rational meaning only. But in the biblical revelation, word is always power and life.[8]

God's Word has power. God does not request that Satan leave. He commands. Scripture declares us to be the temple of the Holy Spirit, which means Satan has no place here. Baptism accomplishes this without having to specifically declare it to be so. The Holy Spirit will take up residence through the simple, yet profound, washing through water and God's Word of promise.

Nevertheless, the purpose is not to do more than what Baptism already does. That is beyond our capabilities. What we seek to do here is to help the church comprehend the fullness of God's gracious work taking place here at the font. A renunciation simply does not capture the sense

---

7. Kolb et al., *The Book of Concord*, 373.
8. Schmemann, *Of Water and the Spirit*, 21, 24. Italics in original.

of what Jesus does in His ministry. Jesus does not request or cajole. He commands and casts out. Evil spirits do not want to leave. As Luther stated earlier, Baptism makes an enemy of Satan and is not something to be taken lightly. With that line of thinking, emphasizing the power of God's declarative Word over demons can only reinforce the might and authority of the Creator in both claiming and protecting His creature.

God loves His children and does not want them to suffer under the weight of Satan's attacks. Moreover, He wants to be that which gives them life so they may live to eternity. Rather than leave it to be a question in the heart of the baptized, repeating God's promise of ownership and His declaration against His demonic enemies leaves no doubt as to who is in charge and what Satan must do now. This reassurance builds on what Baptism is already doing, making explicit the power of God to save His people from any and all enemies.

LIGHTING OF THE CANDLE

The lighting of the baptismal candle is a more recent addition to the baptismal liturgy. In the early church, where Baptism was conducted in the context of Easter, light would have already been a major feature of the feast day. Nowadays, when Baptisms might be conducted on any Sunday of the year, or any day of the week for that matter, the lights and celebration that would normally accompany the Sacrament are generally absent.

Trying to recapture a bit of that Easter light for Baptisms on other days is a major force for the use of candles in modern baptismal rites. The candle becomes another way of communicating what the white garment is also doing. In both cases, the message being conveyed is putting on Christ. With the white garment, it is a visible sign of whose righteousness you now bear. With the candle, the emphasis is on the restored image of God. When the Father looks at a sinner, He sees only darkness, for nothing is given back. When the Father looks at a baptized Christian, He sees the reflection of the One who is the Light. This recalls Christ's own words in Matthew 5: "You are the light of the world. A city set on a hill cannot be hidden. Nor do people light a lamp and put it under a basket, but on a stand, and it gives light to all in the house. In the same way, let your light shine before others, so that they may see your good works and give glory to your Father who is in heaven" (vv. 14–16).

As the moon reflects the sun's light both back to it and to the rest of the world, so now the Christian receives the Son's light and reflects it back to God and to the world. The candle becomes a visible reminder of the light that is given in Baptism. This light is not self-generated. Just as we have no power in ourselves to give life, even to our own body, we also have no power to reflect anything if not for the power of Christ.

The candle has a second baptismal connection as well. John the Baptist remarks how he baptizes with water, but One is coming who will baptize with the Holy Spirit and with fire. As Jesus prepares for His Ascension, He tells the disciples to wait in Jerusalem for the Holy Spirit. Pentecost becomes the fulfillment of that promise as the disciples receive the Holy Spirit and "tongues as of fire" (Acts 2:3).

In the Pentecost event, the fire marks both the power of the Spirit and the fact that He has arrived in that power. Schmemann clarified earlier how Baptism does not mark the reception of particular individual gifts of the Spirit, but rather the Spirit Himself. The fire of Pentecost indicates the Spirit has come and is in their presence to strengthen and empower them on their mission. Here the disciples fulfill their vocation as disciples and begin to enter into a new vocation, that of apostleship.

In this way, the fire is the symbol of the Spirit's presence. The fire is the emblem of the disciple fulfilling her vocation. While no Christian ever ceases to be a disciple, with the gift of the Holy Spirit, the Christian can now embark on his journey of apostleship, which finds its goal and *telos* in the Eucharist.

THE CREED

On par with the sign of the cross, the Creed has been a major part of the baptismal rite since it was developed. Being baptized in the name of the triune God implies an understanding of who that God is and what He asks of us. At the end of Luke 9, Jesus is interacting with several would-be disciples. He says to the last one, "No one who puts his hand to the plow and looks back is fit for the kingdom of God" (v. 62). The Creed represents that acknowledgment.[9]

---

9. In the Western Church, the Apostles' Creed has always been the one associated with Baptism. In the Eastern Church, the Nicene Creed is used in the baptismal rite. In the sense of an acknowledgment of the faith, both creeds work similarly.

Reciting the Creed represents a declaration that I know the God I want to follow. At the end of Joshua's life, he reminds the Israelites of what God has done.

> Now therefore fear the Lord and serve Him in sincerity and in faithfulness. Put away the gods that your fathers served beyond the River and in Egypt, and serve the Lord. And if it is evil in your eyes to serve the Lord, choose this day whom you will serve, whether the gods your fathers served in the region beyond the River, or the gods of the Amorites in whose land you dwell. But as for me and my house, we will serve the Lord . . .
>
> But Joshua said to the people, "You are not able to serve the Lord, for He is a holy God. He is a jealous God; He will not forgive your transgressions or your sins. If you forsake the Lord and serve foreign gods, then He will turn and do you harm and consume you, after having done you good." And the people said to Joshua, "No, but we will serve the Lord." Then Joshua said to the people, "You are witnesses against yourselves that you have chosen the Lord, to serve Him." And they said, "We are witnesses." (Josh. 24:14–15, 19–22)

Though we cannot choose God without His making such a choice possible, by the power of the Spirit that choice is ours to make. We are given the option of staying with the God who has blessed us and redeemed us or going our own way. In Baptism we reject Satan and everything associated with him. We reject our past life of sin and actively seek the righteousness of Christ.

Rejecting Satan and pledging to follow God as His disciple entails knowing who the God is we are going to be following. In rejecting Satan and professing our faith, we are simultaneously rejecting pantheistic concepts of gods, as well the Jewish and Muslim concepts of god. We profess and are saved by a God who reveals Himself and is present in three persons, each of whom are the same God and yet distinct. We believe and trust in a God who has become incarnate and lived in the world with us in the person of Christ.

Our Baptism is necessarily in the name of the triune God, for it is He alone who saves. Without a creedal statement of our faith, we are in danger of misconstruing what we are becoming a part of through our Baptism. The Creed clarifies not only whom we are becoming disciples of but also that this discipleship is lifelong. The triune God is claiming us for eternity, and, by the help of the Spirit, we are claiming Him. Through the Spirit we become the community—the church—we confess to be. Luther adds, "This is the meaning and substance of this phrase: I believe that there is on earth a holy little flock and community of pure saints under one head, Christ. It is called together by the Holy Spirit in one faith, mind, and understanding" (LC II).[10] The work of the Spirit in Baptism is evident. The sign of the Spirit's work in claiming us and bringing us into that holy community is found in Baptism and it is this we confess in the Creed.

The Creed is usually a series of questions just prior to the Baptism proper. Like a child that learns language by repeating his parents, the Christian who is about to be reborn is learning to speak truth by hearing it again from those who already know it. The Christian is about to enter the waters that are inhabited by the Spirit, and the Spirit knows truth when He hears it. The Spirit will make this Christian a prophet again, whose duty will be to speak God's truth about God's work in past, present, and future. No Christian simply has truth. It must be given to us. Schmemann speaks to this transition:

Now the knowledge *about* Christ is to become knowledge *of* Christ; the truth preserved by the Church in her Tradition is to become the faith and life of the new member of the Church. It is for this reason that even today when the whole congregation recites or sings the Creed, it begins not with "We believe" but with "I believe." The Church is a body, an organism, but an organism made up of persons and of their personal commitments. The entire faith is given to each, and each one is responsible for the whole faith.[11]

So here the pastor recites the Creed so the Christian has something to say to the world. Thus, the prophetic vocation begins and the Christian is able to leave the font with a firsthand experience of the truth of the triune God with which to engage the unbelieving world.

THE LORD'S PRAYER

Though a staple of Christian life, the Lord's Prayer has a special place in the baptismal rite in particular. Though many Christians learn the Lord's Prayer very early, it is not until Baptism that this prayer attains its full force.

Prior to Baptism, a Christian prays the prayer without a mature understanding of what it accomplishes. This prayer is woven into Christian

---

10. Kolb et al., *The Book of Concord*, 437.
11. Schmemann, *Of Water and the Spirit*, 33. Italics in original.

life and everything the church does. The prayer contains, in short form, everything a Christian needs. However, it is also everything the world around us needs. Once a Christian has been baptized and enters into the vocation of priest he was meant to have, the Christian begins to pray this prayer in a new way. Not only are baptized Christians praying for their own needs but now they are living out their vocation. The Lord's Prayer becomes their first real act as priests before God.

They may not be thinking in those terms yet, but it is nevertheless true. What before their priestly anointing was "Give me this day my daily bread" can now truly be said "Give us . . . " "Lead me not into temptation . . . " becomes "Lead us . . . " and so forth. For those baptized as infants, they will probably never remember a time when they were not fulfilling their priestly vocation. Nevertheless, the authority to pray this prayer as Jesus gave it to be prayed stems from our priestly anointing in Baptism. This is what allows us to enter into God's presence and lift up the needs of the world to Him. Without that priestly consecration, we can never fully carry out that duty.

The Lord's Prayer comes into our hearing through the disciples' deceptively simple request "Lord, teach us to pray." This is the very essence of discipleship. The various petitions of the Lord's Prayer bring out this life of discipleship even further. Schmemann says this of the First Petition: "'Hallowed be Thy name'—may everything in the world, beginning with my own life, my deeds, my words be a reflection of this sacred and divine name, which has been revealed and given to us."[12] Luther says something similar in his explanation of the First Petition in the Large Catechism:

> But what is it to pray that his name may become holy? Is it not already holy? Answer: Yes, in its essence it is always holy, but our use of it is not holy. God's name was given to us when we became Christians and were baptized, and so we are called children of God and have the sacraments, through which he incorporates us into himself with the result that everything that is God's must serve for our use (LC III).[13]

Nothing encapsulates the work of the priest as much as praying the Lord's Prayer. A Christian who has been baptized and who has been anointed into the priesthood can now take up the prayer Christ gave His disciples to pray and pray as one of them.

12. Schmemann, *Our Father*, 30.
13. Kolb et al., *The Book of Concord*, 445.

It is usually assumed the Lord's Prayer will be a part of the baptismal rite, and it is in both the Eastern and Western Church. Yet, rarely is it discussed why it is a part of the rite. When the baptismal rite is made a part of the worship service, the Lord's Prayer is already a part of the liturgy. Doing it twice in the same service makes little sense unless we connect it to what is taking place in the baptismal rite. Including the Lord's Prayer in the baptismal rite focuses our attention on the newly consecrated priest in our midst. Like a pastor closing out his ordination service with his brother pastors looking on, the new priest is the voice lifting up the cares of church and world while the rest of the church adds their voices to the chorus. The Christian engages in their first service as priest, one they will continue to offer every time they lift the world up to God in prayer.

INFANT BAPTISM

The Baptism of infants is a topic Luther discussed and the Lutheran church has continued to emphasize. Luther takes it as a given in his baptismal booklet that infants will be baptized.[14] I do not need to re-create the entire line of thinking in favor of infant Baptism. It suffices to say everyone carries the sin of Adam with them. It is a part of them from the moment of their conception. That sin makes them an enemy of God from the very beginning, which means people of every age are equally in need of God's grace. Rather than work through all of that, I will examine instead the issues of discipleship that stem from the modern understanding and practice of infant Baptism. Further, as seen in circumcision, God both expects and commands His gifts to be given to tiny infants who have no way of articulating their faith.

Many Christians in the church have been instructed in the connection between Baptism and the Holy Spirit. The Holy Spirit is active in Baptism and enters into the life of the Christian through the Sacrament. When this work of the Spirit becomes mired in a view of Baptism that sees it as more akin to magic than as true gift, the conclusion that is fostered is that children need Baptism because that is where the Holy Spirit instills faith within them.

The baptismal theology we have investigated shows that faith is already taken as a given when the Christian approaches the baptismal font. Luke tells us John the Baptist knew his Savior before he was even born. It

14. Kolb et al., *The Book of Concord*, 371.

is not a stretch at all to see how unborn children who are a part of the life of the church through their parents, particularly as those parents are active in hearing the Word and in worship, are able to hear and know the voice of their Shepherd.

However, the typical Christian view now is that Baptism brings faith. This leads to a belief in Baptism as a magic spell that will instantly create faith in the child and thereby ensure their salvation. This further leads to treating Baptism as the only thing that needs to be done for their spiritual growth and development. This turns Baptism from a gift from God into a gate to salvation that is controlled by the baptizer. The pastor (or family) now controls when the child comes to faith because he controls when the Baptism will be conducted.

The effect of this belief on the church has been immeasurably devastating.[15] With a child's Baptism completed, the thought is that nothing more needs to be done and the family becomes noticeably absent afterward. In fact, the idea that Baptism guarantees faith fuels the view that nothing more needs to be done. The thought is that they, as parents, have brought their child to the font. They are told with absolute certainty that their child has faith now and is saved. Since that was the goal from the outset, they see themselves as having completed their parental duty and have no further need for the church.

Aside from a mistaken concept of Baptism and its place in Christian life, the newly baptized Christian is robbed of the ability to attain the mark of discipleship. Jesus indicates two things are necessary: teaching and Baptism. Baptism is a requirement to be a disciple of Christ, but teaching is equally important. One cannot be a disciple without being claimed as one by the Teacher and then sitting at His feet to learn from Him. Without this, the life of discipleship is never truly engaged.

This point is not one that is argued by theologians. The church universally agrees that children should be raised in the faith and a brief encounter with God at the baptismal font is simply not what He wants and demands of us. However, on the whole we lack a framework for understanding how

---

15. The effects are seen in the lives of those who are baptized but also in the lives of those who are not. Children who are stillborn, who die before they can be baptized, or who, for whatever reason, never make it to the font, become a terrible crisis for parents. The same flawed thinking that believes a child perfectly safe from all harm because he or she has been baptized also would have us believe a child condemned because he or she was never brought to the font to receive the faith necessary for salvation. This becomes a dreadful burden on the consciences of parents, even those who are active in worship.

to address the issue. Making clear the place of Baptism in relation to faith is of utmost importance. Baptism is not intended to be where faith is instilled. God's Word and Spirit are active there, so it can happen, but that is not its primary purpose.

God can instill faith in Baptism. God can bring salvation to a poor sinful child who needs it so desperately. However, this one brief moment does not constitute a life of discipleship and becomes a very dangerous proposition with eternal consequences. The church may not avoid all misconceptions of Baptism and its place in Christian life, but talking about Baptism in the larger context of discipleship and how teaching and Baptism must go together may help steer the church back on course and raise the baptismal rite out of the murky realm of magic and up to the level of the Holy Sacrament it is meant to be.

THE NAMING

Giving the name of the Christian who has come for Baptism is usually the first thing that happens in a baptismal rite. While christening is not a major part of the modern church in Western society, since children rarely make it to Baptism without having a name, the theology behind it is still very applicable.

The theology of naming is threaded throughout the Old Testament. In all cases, it is a part of the vocation of king and ruler. As God gives Adam kingship over creation, his first act as king is to name all the creatures in it. Each creature receives a name that is appropriate to it and marks it as unique. The name given to each creature is a blessing and indicates their participation in the larger community.

God takes this same idea and amplifies it. Jacob becomes Israel. Abram becomes Abraham. In these cases, God is exercising His kingly authority to grant tremendous blessings, and the mark of those blessings is the name which He attaches to them. Abraham and Israel become open displays of God's graciousness, and the names they have been given become associated with the blessings and promises God has granted.

In the case of a Christian who is coming to the font, there is little expectation that their name will change. Infants coming to the font may have only had their names a couple of days. Nevertheless, those coming to the font are coming to be reborn. This means their name needs to be attached to this new life they are leading.

Poor, sinful parents carry out their royal duty and privilege to the best of their ability, giving their child a name that will suit him or her and be the most basic part of their child's identity. But we are conceived in sin and we are named in sin. God's act of naming is ultimately redemptive and Jesus cleanses every part of who we are. That means even the very thing that is used to identify us from the myriads of other people in the world is also in need of cleansing.

And so our name is given that Christ may append His own name to it. Schmemann discusses this in the context of the Orthodox baptismal rite:

> The rite of naming is therefore the acknowledgement by the Church of the *uniqueness* of this particular child, of the divine gift of "personality" to him. By referring it to God's Holy Name, the Church reveals each name to be *holy*, i.e. sanctified by the human name of Christ Himself. In Christ the name of each human being is shown to be the name of a child of God, created and destined for a *personal* relationship with God, a personal participation in God's eternal Kingdom, and not for dissolution in some impersonal "nirvana."[16]

As we become part of the church, we are part of God's family. His name becomes ours as we are formally adopted and become brothers and sisters of Christ, sons and daughters of the Heavenly Father. As parents give their children a name out of the loving familial relationship that binds them, so too our heavenly Father participates in that naming by calling us His own child. In essence, the celebrant acts as the adoption agent, informing God of the name of the new child He is about to adopt.

THE FONT

The baptismal font is usually a centerpiece in any church, surpassed only by the altar itself. In the early church after the popularization of Christianity and the building of dedicated church buildings, Baptisms were typically done in a building designed specifically for the rite. They would typically have a pool with artwork drawing on all the various baptismal themes. This allowed the new Christians to be immersed in the water while simultaneously being immersed in the biblical accounts that give the foundation for the blessings they were about to receive. Prior to the nationalization of Christianity, Baptism would be done anywhere that permitted it.

16. Schmemann, *Of Water and the Spirit*, 139. Italics in original.

Since infant Baptisms are more the norm in the modern world, baptistries have become less important and the rite focused more and more on small areas suitable for infants. The theology of Baptism centers on this space as the place where the triune God will enter the world in ways that will upend everything we understand about that world. As such, the font and the space it occupies should do their best to reflect the awesome work God accomplishes there.

Baptisms out in nature are relatively rare, but certainly can emphasize the re-creation that takes place in the Sacrament. As the Christian is baptized and assumes his kingly and priestly roles once more, creation itself benefits. A Baptism outdoors becomes the earthly king returning to his throne in the world.

More often, Baptisms are done in the church, gathered around the font. While there is nothing that says what must be done for a baptismal font or the space that surrounds it, there is much that can be said about what others have tried to communicate through the construction and placement of the font.

The theological connection between Baptism, Communion, and Christian life are approached in various ways. Often churches will place the font just inside the sanctuary or even in the narthex leading into the sanctuary as a way of communicating how Baptism is the entrance into the presence of God, particularly as found in the Lord's Supper. Placing the font down the aisle in line with the altar shows how Baptism naturally leads to the greater fulfillment found in Communion.

With the construction of the font itself, the most common design used is the octagon. Bringing the eighth day into the baptismal rite in a visible way is something many churches find beneficial for the understanding of the Sacrament. Many times the sides will have depictions of the days of creation, followed by the eighth day resurrection, or of various elements that feed into our baptismal theology. Outside of the octagon, few shapes have any major consensus, though anything that makes a connection to Baptism would be preferred to something that does not. A twelve-sided figure, for instance, might have depictions of the twelve disciples, indicating the one receiving Baptism is becoming one of their number. Sometimes, especially in much larger churches, the font is connected to a baptismal pool so that Baptism may be conducted in either.

Another element in the construction and placement of the font that might not be so readily apparent is the decision on a fixed versus a movable font. For some congregations, a movable font is the only option. Whether because the congregation does not have its own dedicated space, placement issues, or whatever the case may be, a fixed font simply does not work. It is unfortunate that these circumstances arise, but the Spirit is still active in abundance even here. The other unfortunate side effect, especially when a fixed font is possible but was opted against, is the idea that Baptism is not central to Christian life.

With a moveable font, the font usually gets pulled out when there is a Baptism and then is put back in a corner when the Baptism is done. It is out of sight and gets forgotten. The visual effect of having the font in the midst of the church's worship life is lost. The font's very impermanence communicates something about the function it serves and the rite that is done in connection with it. Whether Baptisms are a common event in the congregation or not, the very presence of the font that the congregation must engage with, even if just to walk around it, makes clear the importance of the Sacrament and its purpose in the church.

The importance of the font should also factor into what the font is constructed from and whatever artistic additions might be made to it. The font symbolizes and facilitates one of the most important events in Christian life. Its use should not be one of pure practicality. Its place within the life of the local church and the message it is able to convey can do much to help Baptism integrate into that ongoing life and build understanding of what God is undertaking in and through the Sacrament.

ASPERSION

The aspersion rite is rarely seen in most Lutheran congregations. Catholic and Orthodox churches make much more use of this. Sprinkling the congregation with water recalls the washing they received in Baptism. It is sometimes connected with an Easter Vigil service, recalling all the baptismal theology that the early church associated with the same event.

The rite has its biblical basis in Psalm 51. The psalm reads as an Old Testament cry for Baptism. It calls for more than just forgiveness: also cleansing and restoration. The aspersion rite does not renew Baptism but rather brings our Baptism back to mind, reminding us of what we have received. The psalmist calls out for a clean heart and a right spirit, for the ability to offer a proper sacrifice. All of these are baptismal in nature. The psalmist calls for the very thing God later provides through the baptismal font and gives to His people.

Participating in the rite of aspersion becomes both a time of solemn reflection and quiet celebration. We remember why Baptism is necessary, silently crying out as King David does, with our sin ever before us. We are broken and corrupt beings who are unable to even offer God anything. Then, through the restorative waters of Baptism, we are made new and whole again. Everything David asks for is done for us. We are given new hearts and spirits. We are given the ability to offer proper sacrifices to God once again.

Now that we have received the gift of Baptism, we celebrate that we have received new hearts and spirits and have been restored. In the context of Easter Vigil, it directs our attention toward the true celebration of Easter. In other liturgical contexts the theme may vary, but it is all oriented toward moving from our broken state toward our restored state, and Baptism is the means by which that happens. Aspersion helps us to see how we have been moved from the former to the latter and that this is the new status we are given.

ONGOING CONSIDERATIONS

Much of this section has been aimed at individual aspects of the baptismal rite and the things immediately associated with it. Hopefully the thoughts conveyed here provide you with new ways of considering the implications of Baptism and how it connects to your life and the life of the church.

However, even if all these ideas are implemented and are beneficial for the spiritual life of the congregation, the goal is to bring Baptism into the weekly and even daily life of the church. If everything said about Baptism and its relationship to time is true, then our Baptism is actively directing us away from this world and everything associated with it and moving us toward the next.

This is a constant process. God's restorative power is infiltrating our sin-plagued bodies every moment and through us is beginning to revivify the world. As such, it is the church's responsibility to help reinforce the work of Baptism throughout the lives of all its members. The pastor's job to preach and teach Baptism is one obvious source of reinforcement, but there may be many more. Each church is a part of the Body of Christ, but each is also unique, with unique local history and traditions. Finding ways to incorporate baptismal themes into the ongoing life of the church will help baptismal theology to flow into the teaching side of discipleship, as well as foster the transition to apostleship.

How this is done will depend very much on the life of the local congregation. Announcing and celebrating baptismal birthdays is a way to keep Baptism fresh in the minds of the congregation and to remember that we continue to live out our Baptisms every day. A baptismal banner that includes the names of everyone who has been baptized in the congregation is a way of showing how the church fosters these Christians by caring for them and lifting them to God. It demonstrates that the church plays a role in creating disciples and helps the church to see how its work is a benefit to God's kingdom. Simply including artwork in the church that carries baptismal themes will also help those various themes to connect in the daily life of the church.

Some congregations will have the font open and full of water on a regular basis. This is usually taught as a way to help the congregation to see their Baptism as continuing and active. Some members will dip their fingers into it to make the sign of the cross. This is most effective when the font is positioned near the entryway into the sanctuary. It must be emphasized that this is not meant to act like holy water in the Catholic Church. Each Christian's Baptism is sufficient and needs nothing added to it. If used, this is simply a way of helping each Christian remember his or her status as a baptized and redeemed child of God.

However a congregation chooses to integrate Baptism into its life, it is something that should be given the priority Baptism is due. As I stated in the introduction, the church has lost the sense of what Baptism is and what it is for. Thus, any method that can be used to help the congregation and each individual to better appropriate the richness of God's gift can only benefit the life of discipleship God has given His people to live.

11

The Worship Service—Where Disciples are Trained

BEFORE ALL THE BIBLE studies, the outreach programs, and community service projects a church might engage in to build up the kingdom, the worship service is first and foremost where disciples are trained. Everything about it is there to teach those who are looking forward to Baptism or taking those who have been baptized and helping them to live out the restored vocations they are given in the Sacrament.

Schmemann says:

> Liturgical catechesis shows us first of all the main *purpose,* the aim of religious education as it is understood by the Church. This aim is *to bring the individual into the life of the Church* . . . Religious education is nothing else but the disclosing of that which happened to man when he was born again through water and Spirit, and was made a *member of the Church.*[1]

The task of discipleship is ongoing and Christian life both begins and is focused on the time we spend in the presence of God. It is here we grow into the people He has made us to be.

We have already looked at how some of the feast days of the liturgical year can be beneficial times for connecting with Baptism. Teaching the significance of the liturgical cycle is also important for beginning to act out the role of disciple we have been given. Each year we are invited to follow Christ's life again. He reminds us why He came and what He has done for

1. Schmemann, *Liturgy and Life*, 11. Italics in original.

The Worship Service—Where Disciples Are Trained

us. We hear what He says and see how He acts. As children who learn by watching their parents, we as disciples learn by watching our Master.

The first half of the worship service, centering on the proclamation and exposition of the Word, is geared toward building up disciples in the study of Christ and His life. By hearing the Gospel, people also hear that they are continuing in their Baptism. Their sins are still being washed clean. They also continue to learn about the work of Christ in the world. They have a new piece of His life to guide them each week and to focus their attention. Thus, the liturgical year weaves its way through the service and encourages the disciples to walk in the footsteps of Christ each week.

The proclamation of the Word is central to baptismal life, and so that proclamation is central to the service. Without this focus on the Word, the service is missing one of the most essential pieces. That also means the structure and content of the service are meant to reinforce the work of the Word and inform us on how to put the Word into action. The hymnody and the liturgical text surrounding the Scripture are all meant to build on the message and give it further shape, to bring the church into the life of Christ. The liturgical texts are primarily drawn directly from Scripture and the hymnody takes the themes and events of Scripture and puts them to music. All this fits together into a cohesive whole so the Christian can step into the life of the disciples as they follow Jesus and learn to live as He has called them to live.

A large part of the discipleship that takes place in the service is in the actions that are carried out. It is not so much a matter of the actions being done but rather why they are being done and who is doing them. The prayers in the service are a primary example. We have already looked at the Lord's Prayer as the quintessential work of a priest before God. However, all the other prayers in the service follow the same idea. The Collect of the Day takes the Scripture reading and calls on God to make good on the promises contained within it and to continue the activity that had been started in the life of Christ. The Prayers of the Church lift up the concerns of the local church, the church around the world, and earthly concerns of the world as a whole.

Rather than being just something the church does, these prayers are the unique and special domain of the holy priesthood. Christians are called to follow in the footsteps of our great High Priest, Christ Jesus, and are the ones who carry on the priestly work as He taught. Since our priestly consecration comes through Baptism, it becomes an integral part of Christian life. Thus, praying in all these different ways and about these different things teaches us what it means to be priests. We call God's attention to His covenant promises, such as the rainbow after the Flood. The prayers of a priest are for the individual, for others, and for all creation. Creation has no voice to speak its cares and concerns. It needs mankind to function as priests so that God hears creation and responds appropriately. This is what a priest is meant to do and the worship service is where we begin carrying out that role. Some of this is also a reflection of our kingly duty to care for creation as well. It is only by knowing what the needs of creation are that those needs can be lifted up to God.

We also discussed the role of the Creed in the baptismal rite. We speak the Creed as we learn what it means to speak the truth and what truth we are to speak. Every Sunday we continue that training, practicing our prophetic vocation as we claim the entirety of God's Word as our own once more and prepare ourselves to share that Word with the world as Christ commands in the Great Commission.

The offerings we give, whatever form they take, are a continuation of the priestly role as we offer to God a portion of what He has given us. Again, the priestly duty is the focal point as God is honored and the work of the kingdom supported.

In much of the early church period, when Baptism was primarily for adults and usually only happened once or twice a year, Christians would attend worship for quite a while before being baptized. Great care was taken to educate the newly faithful before they received the Sacrament. In those days, when the service transitioned to Communion, those who had not yet been baptized were asked to leave. It was thought they were not ready to understand the holy mystery of Communion and certainly not ready to participate.

The Word begins our faith, which Baptism then takes and builds up into the role of disciple. However, it is Communion that is the goal of Christian life. This is where God becomes physically present with His people. We are reminded of what allowed Aaron and the subsequent high priests to approach God in the Most Holy Place to offer the appropriate sacrifices. It is only by being made clean and holy that they were fit to enter that space. We, too, are made holy through Baptism, so every Sunday is a constant reminder of our status as holy and consecrated as we approach Almighty God at His table.

The Worship Service—Where Disciples are Trained

The liturgy brings all this together so that we hear who God has made us and then begin living out what we have been made. Without the liturgy to help train us as disciples, our efforts would be bumbling and ineffectual. We would have no model to emulate and no concept of what the life of a disciple looks like. Instead, the worship service, where God's Word and Sacraments are found, is the place where disciples are made and trained. The life of disciples is not contained solely in the worship service, but this is where they begin to take on that role in earnest.

Conclusion

THE IMMENSITY OF BAPTISM's impact on individual Christian lives and on the church as a whole can be seen throughout Scripture. God spends so much of the Old Testament teaching and preparing the world for what will later take place through the life of Christ. Together with the pure Word of God, the Sacraments constitute the greatest gifts God has given. As such, they form the trunk of the theological tree which grows up out of the root which is Christ Himself. Everything the church does stems from these three things in one way or another.

Many of the theological battles Luther and the reformers fought during the Reformation revolved around the Sacraments and their use. Though those discussions may not be happening with the same frequency or intensity between the various branches of Christendom these days, those debates did happen because all involved understood the importance of understanding the purpose of the Sacraments.

If so much of the Bible can be directed at informing us about what God is doing through Baptism, then it is imperative that the church take that message seriously and dedicate the necessary time and energy to its study. Without a deeper understanding of the Sacrament, the church will never put into practice the full measure of grace it has been given and will only ever fulfill its vocation in a stumbling and infantile way. When the church is struggling with issues of discipleship and helping members to deepen their faith, the first place to look is back at the two things that create disciples: teaching and Baptism. For discipleship to be a daily feature of Christian life, that teaching must continue. Receiving the gift of Baptism is what takes place as the Christian comes to the font, but that gift is not meant to be looked at and set aside. It is meant to be unwrapped and examined from all angles. It is meant to be explored to its depths and for all of its brilliance to bring delight. It is meant to be cherished. For it to truly be the

CONCLUSION

gift of love it is meant to be, the church must fully comprehend how much work God put in so that He could offer it to each of us freely.

That Baptism functions as a means of grace is what establishes it as a sacrament. To look at Baptism in any other context is to draw it out of the framework that was designed to hold it all together. At the same time, the grace conveyed by Baptism is meant to have form and function. Like a tidal wave falling on the shore, the baptismal waters crash into our lives and our lives should be irrevocably changed. The grace of God flows through all these different themes and fills them with the power to effect change.

All these themes swirl around the rite of Baptism and come out variously in response to the life of the church and the individual. All are present all the time, but which one comes to the fore depends on a myriad of factors such as the liturgical season, the spiritual life of the individual, and so forth. A Baptism that takes place during the Christmas or Epiphany seasons may use the lighting of the candle to draw on the idea of Christ as the light of the world. A Baptism during the Pentecost season may use that same rite to draw on the Holy Spirit's blessing of the disciples on Pentecost. Both are perfectly valid and a theme that is stronger at one point may later give way to a different theme as God continues to converse with His church and attend to its needs.

The wealth of biblical imagery and meaning behind Baptism gives the church an endless fountain with which to confront sin and offer God's gracious restoration. The forgiveness given in Baptism does so much more than we might first expect. It is an endless, ever-present gift from God that strikes us differently every time we contemplate its richness. With the wealth of baptismal grace to meditate on, we will never cease to find God's consolation and wisdom wherever we find ourselves in life.

Bibliography

Daniélou, Jean. 1956. The Bible and the Liturgy. Notre Dame: University of Notre Dame Press.
Kolb, Robert, Timothy J. Wengert, and Charles P. Arand. 2000. The Book of Concord: The Confessions of the Evangelical Lutheran Church. Minneapolis, MN: Fortress.
Luther, Martin. 1999. Luther's Works, Vol. 1: Lectures on Genesis: Chapters 1–5. Edited by Jaroslav Jan Pelikan, Hilton C. Oswald and Helmut T. Lehmann. Vol. 1. Saint Louis: Concordia Publishing House.
———. 1999. Luther's Works, Vol. 2: Lectures on Genesis: Chapters 6–14. Edited by Jaroslav Jan Pelikan, Hilton C. Oswald and Helmut T. Lehmann. Vol. 2. Saint Louis: Concordia Publishing House.
———. 1999. Luther's Works, Vol. 3: Lectures on Genesis: Chapters 15–20. Edited by Jaroslav Jan Pelikan, Hilton C. Oswald and Helmut T. Lehmann. Vol. 3. Saint Louis: Concordia Publishing House.
———. 1999. Luther's Works, Vol. 9: Lectures on Deuteronomy. Edited by Jaroslav Jan Pelikan, Hilton C. Oswald and Helmut T. Lehmann. Vol. 9. Saint Louis: Concordia Publishing House.
———. 1999. Luther's Works, Vol. 19: Minor Prophets II: Jonah and Habakkuk. Edited by Jaroslav Jan Pelikan, Hilton C. Oswald and Helmut T. Lehmann. Vol. 19. Saint Louis: Concordia Publishing House.
———. 1999. Luther's Works, Vol. 20: Minor Prophets III: Zechariah. Edited by Jaroslav Jan Pelikan, Hilton C. Oswald and Helmut T. Lehmann. Vol. 20. Saint Louis: Concordia Publishing House.
———. 1999. Luther's Works, Vol. 22: Sermons on the Gospel of St. John: Chapters 1–4. Edited by Jaroslav Jan Pelikan, Hilton C. Oswald and Helmut T. Lehmann. Saint Louis: Concordia Publishing House.
———. 1999. Luther's Works, Vol. 23: Sermons on the Gospel of St. John: Chapters 6–8. Edited by Jaroslav Jan Pelikan, Hilton C. Oswald and Helmut T. Lehmann. Vol. 23. Saint Louis: Concordia Publishing House.
———. 1999. Luther's Works, Vol. 24: Sermons on the Gospel of St. John: Chapters 14–16. Edited by Jaroslav Jan Pelikan, Hilton C. Oswald and Helmut T. Lehmann. Vol. 24. Saint Louis: Concordia Publishing House.
———. 1999. Luther's Works, Vol. 27: Lectures on Galatians, 1535, Chapters 5–6; 1519, Chapters 1–6. Edited by Jaroslav Jan Pelikan, Hilton C. Oswald and Helmut T. Lehmann. Vol. 27. Saint Louis: Concordia Publishing House.

Bibliography

———. 1999. Luther's Works, Vol. 29: Lectures on Titus, Philemon, and Hebrews. Edited by Jaroslav Jan Pelikan, Hilton C. Oswald and Helmut T. Lehmann. Vol. 29. Saint Louis: Concordia Publishing House.

———. 1999. Luther's Works, Vol. 30: The Catholic Epistles. Edited by Jaroslav Jan Pelikan, Hilton C. Oswald and Helmut T. Lehmann. Vol. 30. Saint Louis: Concordia Publishing House.

———. 1999. Luther's Works, Vol. 31: Career of the Reformer I. Edited by Jaroslav Jan Pelikan, Hilton C. Oswald and Helmut T. Lehmann. Vol. 31. Philadelphia: Fortress.

———. 1999. Luther's Works, Vol. 35: Word and Sacrament I. Edited by Jaroslav Jan Pelikan, Hilton C. Oswald and Helmut T. Lehmann. Vol. 35. Philadelphia: Fortress.

———. 1999. Luther's Works, Vol. 38: Word and Sacrament IV. Edited by Jaroslav Jan Pelikan, Hilton C. Oswald and Helmut T. Lehmann. Vol. 38. Philadelphia: Fortress.

———. 1999. Luther's Works, Vol. 40: Church and Ministry II. Edited by Jaroslav Jan Pelikan, Hilton C. Oswald and Helmut T. Lehmann. Vol. 40. Philadelphia: Fortress.

———. 1999. Luther's Works, Vol. 54: Table Talk. Edited by Jaroslav Jan Pelikan, Hilton C. Oswald and Helmut T. Lehmann. Vol. 54. Philadelphia: Fortress.

———. 2009. Luther's Works, Vol. 69: Sermons on John 17–20. Edited by Christopher Boyd Brown. Vol. 69. St. Louis: Concordia Publishing House.

Schmemann, Alexander. 1973. For the Life of the World. Crestwood: St. Vladimir's Seminary.

———. 2006. Liturgy and Life: Lectures and Essays on Christian Development Through Liturgical Experience. New York: Dept. of Religious Education, Orthodox Church in America.

———. 1974. Of Water & the Spirit: A Liturgical Study of Baptism. Crestwood: St. Vladimir's Seminary.

———. 2002. Our Father. Crestwood: St. Vladimir's Seminary.

Tertullian, "On Baptism," in *Latin Christianity: Its Founder, Tertullian*, ed. Alexander Roberts, James Donaldson, and A. Cleveland Coxe, trans. S. Thelwall, vol. 3, The Ante-Nicene Fathers (Buffalo, NY: Christian Literature Company, 1885), 669–680.

www.ingramcontent.com/pod-product-compliance
Lightning Source LLC
Chambersburg PA
CBHW070453090426
42735CB00012B/2537